The Selected Poems of
Jean Sénac

The Selected Poems of
Jean Sénac

Translated by Katia Sainson & David Bergman

The Sheep Meadow Press
Riverdale-on-Hudson, NY

Designed and typeset by The Sheep Meadow Press

Distributed by The University Press of New England

All inquiries and permission requests should be addressed to the
publisher:

The Sheep Meadow Press
PO Box 1345
Riverdale, NY 10471

Dérisions et vertiges © Actes Sud, 1983
Le mythe du sperme - Méditerranée © Actes Sud, 1984
Poèmes © Actes Sud, 1989

Library of Congress Cataloging-in-Publication Data

Sénac, Jean, 1926-1973.
 [Poems. English & French. Selections]
 The selected poems of Jean Sénac / translated by Katia Sainson
and David Bergman.
    p. cm.
 ISBN 978-1-931357-75-3
 I. Sainson, Katia. II. Bergman, David, 1950- III. Title.
 PQ3989.S468A2 2009
 841⟩.914--dc22
                                    2009045095

to Jacques, Hamid and the two Johns

Acknowledgments

We owe a great debt of gratitude to both Jacques Miel and Hamid Nacer-Khodja, without whom this volume would not have been possible. We are most grateful for the help of Jacques Miel, Jean Sénac's adoptive son, who opened both his home and his memory to us and without whose support this translation could not have been realized. Our deepest appreciation and admiration go to Hamid Nacer-Khodja, for his unfailing generosity in sharing the fruit of a lifetime of meticulous scholarship, which has been so instrumental in keeping Jean Senac's memory alive. We would also like to thank Jean-François Pinet and all the staff in the Département Patrimoine: Fonds Rares et Précieux at the Bibliothèque Municipale de la Ville de Marseille, Alcazar for all their help in navigating the wealth of material in their collection. Finally, our sincere thanks to Richard Sieburth for his support and wise counsel as well as to Richard Schneider, Jr. for his early interest in this project.

CONTENTS

From *Myth of the Mediterranean Semen* (1967)

From *derision & Vertigo / discovoids* (1967-1972)

From *Plaques* (1973)

From *For a Possible Land*

PREFACE

Salaam to Jean Sénac,
Supreme and Rejected Algerian Poet

by Richard Howard

From our first immersion in Sénac's poetry of excess (for even
this continent selection, so equably sieved and so legitimately
translated, is excessive, immoderate, furiously plethoric); from
the initial infraction of this rapturous aspersion-by-words—

> Here everything is swift seaweed
>   affectionate as secrecy
> Here everything is accurate sand
>   and when you withdraw you hand
>   you recreate your extravagant sea
> Here everything is fragile love
>   made to the sun's dimension
> Here everything is intense breath
>   disorderly exploits
> Here everything is sweating sap
>   his voice as carnal as his dream
> Here everything is made glorious

—we emerge dazed from these depths, we *surface* choking and
gagging on the inexorable inundation of *the wrong language*:

always French, French striving and straining to do the work of Arabic, so that the very justice of an equally inapplicable English deceives the outrage of the gorgeous occidental syllables. And we gasp the "intense breath" this incompatibly francophone Algerian poet could never draw for his country, this illegitimate son of a Spanish woman named *Comma* (that one punctuation mark of modest interspersion invariably exiled from Sénac's utterance which readily dispenses with any punctuation that might bridle, might *chasten* utterance), this repudiated minstrel ultimately abandoned by Camus and Char, his initial poetic masters; this *European Algerian* silenced by the national Revolution of '62 he ecstatically welcomed, murdered by a fundamentalist loathing of his proud homosexuality and his refusal, his incapacity to cancel French and accept a Muslim identity.

Yet read half a dozen poems, especially from the second half of Sénac's immense body of work, say from the waist down (for once the accurate figure of speech), not discarding the immensity of the residue but sipping rather than gulping the ecstatic vintage which welcomes his readers, the same brew prepared by Whitman and Rimbaud, and you will be rewarded by the dress of yet another consummate bard, one more naked Mediterranean *trouvère,* clad in all the redundant rags and riches of his art.

AVANT-PROPOS

Que la poésie, ce tamaris toujours indemne qui éploie sa gra-
cilité sur le rivage et les falaises de la mer, sa racine étroite
logée dans le sol même où les restes des ouvrages fortifiés
des modernes envahisseurs achèvent de se décomposer, que la
poésie, en cette matinée où je l'interroge, triomphe en bloc
m'assurant que la puissance de ses ennemis est éphémère et
leur art voué au néant, c'est assez pour que le visage souverain
d'Ariel soit une fois de plus ressuscité. Doucement les tamaris
s'agitent et des lèvres de lumière rose impriment çà et là le
feuillage pulvérisé.

Les poèmes qui m'accompagnent ici aujourd'hui sont ceux
de Jean Sénac. Ils chantent à longue voix nourrie et pure
le paysage de l'atelier immense du soleil, atelier qui a la nuit
pour toiture et l'homme comme exploit décevant et merveil-
leux. Le vent ami tourne dans mes doigts les pages du cahier
où une écriture de jeune homme s'établit en poésie.

Fortifications pour vivre
René Char

FOREWORD
to Jean Sénac's *Poèmes* (1954)

May poetry—that gracile, unscathed tamarisk on seashore and cliff that unfurls, forcing its narrow roots into the very soil where the remains of fortified works of modern invaders fall into their final stages of decay—triumph unequivocally on this morning as I question it. Thus, I'll be assured that the power of its enemies is ephemeral and that their art is destined for the void. This alone can once again resurrect Ariel's supreme countenance. Gently, the tamarisks stir leaving the imprint of pink-lit lips, here and there, on the pulverized foliage.

Today, the poems that accompany me are Jean Sénac's. They sing in a long, sustained and pure voice of the land where the sun has its workshop— a workshop whose roof is the night and for whom man is a disappointing and marvelous achievement. Through my fingers, the friendly wind turns the pages of the notebook in which a young man's jottings establish themselves as poetry.

Fortifications for living
René Char

INTRODUCTION

by Katia Sainson

In 1973, when the poet Jean Sénac was found dead in his Algiers basement-apartment, the victim of what is believed by some to have been a government assassination, he left behind a large body of work. And yet his poetry has often been eclipsed by his dramatic life story and tragic end. This, the first English-language collection of Sénac's work, tracks the evolution of this neglected Algerian author. We begin with his earliest poems when, as a disciple of René Char and Albert Camus, the young poet wrote what he would later describe as "precious knick-knacks,"— rigorously carved verse, reminiscent of his mentor Char.   In the period between 1954 and 1965, Sénac's poetry took a political turn when he became the most important French-language poet associated with Algeria's nationalist circles.   In the final years of his life, one of the rare *pieds-noirs*[1] to have stayed on post-independence, he found his voice as an openly-gay advocate of political and personal freedom.   During this late period, his poems, which could be alternately economical or unbridled, combined the raw orality of Ginsberg's *Howl* with the lyricism of Pasolini's civic poetry.

Sénac was born in 1926 in Béni-Saf, Algeria, the illegitimate son of Jeanne Comma, who was of Spanish origin. Having never known anything about his father, who his mother implied had raped her, he took the surname of the

---

1 The term used to designate French Settlers in Algeria

Frenchman, Edmond Sénac, who married and soon divorced Jean's mother.

If his illegitimacy and his obsession with "inhabiting a name" was a constant source of tension in his life as well as a recurring theme in his work the same can be said about nationality. He always called himself an Algerian. However, as a pied-noir with ties to the FLN (the Front de libération national) that fought to overthrow France's colonial rule, and, later, as an adult living in a post-colonial Algeria that did not grant citizenship to non-Muslim natives, he always grappled with being an outsider because of his European descent. Despite his wholehearted alignment on the side of those fighting for Algerian independence, he was often accused both during and after the war of having no business participating in the struggle of this population, which was predominantly Arab, Berber and Muslim. Sénac, the *gaouri*, a term for a foreigner or infidel commonly used in Algeria, struggled against criticism for "not being Arab and for not being named Mohamed Ben Senaq."[2]

This volume represents only a small selection of Sénac's prolific poetic production. We begin with poems from the author's first published collection *Poems* (1954), published by Gallimard with the support of two of the towering intellectual influences and father-figures in his life, René Char and Albert Camus. While the young poet clearly pays homage to Camus in the poem entitled "Noces"—after Camus' early collection of essays of that same title—it is René Char's influence that is most present in his early work. As the Algerian-born Gabriel Audisio wrote to Sénac regarding these poems: "You know the secret, even if at times, it's obvious that it was passed on to you by another magician."[3]

2 Rachid Boudjedra: *Lettres algériennes*, (Paris: Grasset, 1995), p.74.
3 Letter to Sénac from Audisio, from April 5, 1954 in the Sénac archives in Marseille.

With the poems from *My People's Early Rising [Matinale de mon people]* from 1961, Sénac begins to define his own poetic voice. These poems were written between 1954 and 1961 during the Algerian War, when Sénac was in self-imposed exile in France. The collection brings together the nationalist, militant poems for which he is perhaps most remembered in Algeria. These are the poems that were taught in Algerian classrooms and included in anthologies in the years immediately after independence. In the poems from this collection, such as "Homeland," "Faraway Algiers," "Bearers of News" and "Salute to Black Writers and Artists"—a poem that Camus called "unacceptable, indecent, and shameful"—Sénac invokes the names of important figures in the Algerian War such as Djamila Bouhired, Henri Alleg, and Larbi Ben M'Hidi, as well as the long struggle of anonymous Algerians who were attempting to throw off the colonial system.

This is also the period when Sénac breaks off what had been his close and intense relationship with the man he had alternately referred to as his brother, friend, lover and most frequently, as his father—Albert Camus. The relationship began in 1947, when a young Sénac, then in a sanatorium in Rivet, wrote an admiring letter to Camus, who by that time, had already achieved literary fame. When the young poet first came to France, Camus offered him both financial and professional help. As Sénac became more involved in the nationalist movement, however, tension grew between the two men. Like many of Camus's admirers, Sénac urged him to raise his voice, both exacting and honest, to plead the Algerian cause. By 1957 Sénac complained about "the awful name that for the last year Camus takes pleasure in greeting me with— *cut-throat*," referring no doubt to the common FLN practice of slitting the throats of their victims. The poet even wrote "A Albert Camus qui me traitait d'égorgeur" [To Albert Camus who called me a cut-throat] a poem he never published and in which he condemns the "Master of the Absolute" with his politics of clean hands.

The relationship finally ended, in 1958, at the time that Camus, who had just been awarded the Nobel Prize for Literature in Stockholm made several statements trying to explain his silence on Algeria. Most famously Camus stated in a meeting with students in Stockholm that although "I believe in justice, I shall defend my mother above justice." Sénac could not accept this from an author who had once sung the praises of the "Just" engaged in violent struggle, and in a note written in 1958 the poet answers: "Camus was my father. Having to choose between my father and justice, I have chosen justice." Shortly after, the two men saw each other for the last time before the Nobel laureate's death in an automobile accident in 1960.

In 1962, while most of the pieds-noirs in Algeria were leaving the newly independent land in a mass exodus, Sénac returned to his country from which he had been separated during the eight years of the war in order to participate in its rebuilding. In those early years Sénac's Algeria was a place dominated by the charismatic populist Ahmed Ben Bella, who rose to power after what would be the first of many power struggles between 1962 and 1965. He promoted his own brand of socialism, in which he called for *l'autogestion* or self-management, reforestation, and agricultural reform. Along with the hopes of an equitable redistribution of wealth, many aspired to bring about a pluralistic Algeria reminiscent of the Algeria envisioned, in the prewar era, by Camus. In 1961, Sénac proclaimed in an unpublished piece addressed to the European population of the former colony "all Algerians will be free and have equal rights [...] in a secular, democratic and social republic. [We will live] together, without barriers. [Our] two communities will eventually fuse into one."[4]

4 *Pieds-noirs mes frères* in *Poésie au Sud : Jean Sénac et la nouvelle poésie algérienne d'expression française* (Marseille : Archives de la ville de Marseille, 1983)

Sénac, who never learned Arabic and who promoted the work of French language poets as well as Arabic-language poets in Algeria, was a passionate supporter of Ben Bella's government. Upon his return to Algiers in October 1962 he played official roles: advisor to the Minister of Education and a founder and general secretary of the Union of Algerian Writers, where he would remain until he was forced to resign due to political pressure in 1966. More importantly, Sénac's status as an Algerian cultural icon was solidified not by these official positions, but rather by his role as the host of two extremely popular radio programs, broadcast on Algerian State Radio between 1963 and 1972. These programs emphasized contemporary world poetry including the works of American poets Ginsberg and Whitman, Spanish poets Lorca, Cernuda, Blas de Otero, and Turkish poet Nazim Hikmet. He featured emerging poets from the Third World as well as hundreds of verses sent in, on a weekly basis, from listeners from around the country. In those early years of the new republic, Sénac continued to produce unabashedly patriotic odes that offered unquestioning approval of the new regime, such as his "Aux Héros purs" [To Pure Heroes] (1962) or "Citoyens de Beauté" [Citizens of Beauty] (1963)—that was written after Che Guevara's visit to Algeria with the oft-quoted (and ridiculed) verse "tu es belle comme une comité de gestion" [you are as beautiful as a worker's management committee].

However, as Algeria battled to define its new identity it was unclear whether it would be a multiethnic, multicultural and multiracial state. In the context of the rise of Arab nationalism, which took its lead from Nasser's Egypt, Ben Bella's new Algeria promoted arabisation and islamisation. Even the most ardent supporters of independence began to question the direction that the new nation was taking. It is at this time, with his collection *Citizens of Beauty* (1967) that Sénac begins the renewal of his writing style that will produce the fully realized poetic voice of the works written in the last six years of his

life. Here we find poems that fuse the themes of revolutionary fervor with that of physical desire: "Arbatache," and of course, "Dirge for a Gaouri"—Sénac's ode to his undimmed vision for a new multicultural Algeria in which he predicts his own fate as a victim of this increasingly exclusionary regime.

In 1966 and 1967 Sénac distanced himself from the political arena. He produced the poems that would eventually be published in *Fore-body* [*Avant-Corps*], (1968) and *Myth of the Mediterranean-Semen* [*Mythe du sperme-Méditerranée*] (published posthumously in 1984). With its hauntingly beautiful "Iliac Poems," its recurring variations on the biblical story of Jacob wrestling with the Angel at Jabbok's Ford and its exploration of, what for Sénac, were the almost exclusively erotic connotations of the Arabic letter *noûn* (ن), *Fore-body* is a collection of poems in which Sénac transgresses the taboos of his past and takes an unambiguous and provocative stance against the hypocrisies and intolerance of Algeria's military dictatorship which, after a coup d'état, was now under the control of Houari Boumediène. In these poems he "came out" by unequivocally declaring his love for other men, celebrating his homosexuality in what he called his "corpoems," a coinage that expressed his desire to produce a literature of the body.

In a rare interview with journalist Jean-Pierre Peroncel-Hugoz, Sénac discussed the deliberate linkage of his twin ideals of political and sexual liberation: "*Fore-body* is important for me because if in my wartime poems I confronted the oppressor, in these corpoems I face down alienation by [...] admitting my homosexuality for the first time, in a way that is neither ostentatious nor smug. This is not essential; it is simply one component of my being that, like my socialist convictions, deserves respect."[5] By combining the themes of love and revolution, Sénac is anticipating the tide that would culminate in the student movements of 1968, where the so-

5 Jean-Pierre Peroncel-Hugoz, *Assassinat d'un poète*, (Marseille: Editions du Quai, 1983), 35.

cial revolution that was being called for was inseparable from the sexual revolution that would unleash society's constricted desires.

He continues in this same direction with the poems from *Myth*, which is a book of disillusion that Sénac did not want to publish during his lifetime. We have included all the poems from this short, painful book, which grows out of his increasing sense of isolation.

In the years between 1968 and the end of his life in 1973 Sénac was marginalized as he increasingly clashed with Algeria's military government with its growing ties to fundamentalism. He was forced to resign from his position in the Union of Algerian Writers. Eventually, his popular radio program, Poésie sur tous les fronts, whose listening audience rivaled that of the most popular soap operas and soccer matches, was cancelled. It was during this time, that he had been reduced to living in two small, rat-infested basement rooms on a garbage-strewn courtyard on rue Elisée-Reclus —a place he called his cave. It had been a dizzying downward spiral that led him from his previous apartment—referred to as his balcony on the sea (or BSM, for balcon sur la mer)—on the beach of Pointe-Pescade to this hole where he wrote the poems selected from *derision & Vertigo/discovoids* [dérision & Vertige/trouvures], published posthumously in 1983. At this time when he had lost everything and had become an exile in his own land, he also wrote his most daring and unrestrained poetry. Strikingly, like in so much of the poetry of his later years the poems of this dispossessed and uprooted man, maintain a steadfast optimism as he continued to proclaim the power of social, political and sexual liberation.

His struggle is clear in a 1970 letter to his adopted son Jacques Miel when he writes: "Misery and splendor, derision and Vertigo, I am trying, against the tide and almost as an outlaw, to hold on. It is hard...." And yet, Sénac did not retreat from controversy even during this time when those

closest to him were trying to convince him to leave Algeria. In 1971, he edited *L'Anthologie de la nouvelle poésie algérienne* which showcased the work of young Algerian poets writing in French, at a time when the choice to write in French was viewed as politically suspect. Even as he argues in his preface to the anthology for the creative spark that arabisation will bring to Algerian literature, he defends the linguistic choice of the young poets (and of course his own choice) in a brazenly provocative way: "[These young poets] represent the counter-culture that will be accused of all the flaws of Western civilization, when in fact, quite the contrary, they are continuing in the tradition of great minds which, from Ibn Farid and Abou Nowas to Sidi Boumédiène to Si Mohand, perpetuate a deeply Arabic tradition of love—at once mystical and bisexual—and of freedom. But it is not surprising that the hypocritical and base bourgeoisie that in the past has persecuted [...] and imprisoned [great Arabic poets and intellectuals] is once more bellowing over loud speakers." [6]

Sénac's final collection of poems *Plaques* was written during the last year of his life. In fact several poems were written over the course of a single day, May 24, 1973. These poems, in which the foreboding of his imminent death takes center stage, are tragic and yet at the same time written with a disarmingly light touch.

Sénac was found stabbed to death in his apartment in September 1973 in a brutal murder. But, with his death, it can be argued that his status as a cultural martyr sometimes burns brighter than his poems. Some, who were closest to him, believe his murder could have been the result of a sexual encounter gone wrong. However, for others, Sénac, a popular voice against authoritarianism and exclusionary ideologies, was eliminated because he had become a thorn in the side of

6 *Anthologie de la nouvelle poésie algérienne*, (Paris : Librairie Saint-Germain-des-Près), 35.

those in power. Thus, with his bloody death he became the "first victim of Algerian fundamentalist Islam [...] assassinated by fundamentalists who hated intelligence and the other"[7] —a victim of the ideological clashes that would reach their climax in Algeria's bloody civil strife of the 1990's.

In death, just as in life, Sénac remains an outsider. Although his poetic works and his autobiographical novel *Ebauche du père* were published in France posthumously, Sénac has no place in the French literary cannon, where he is considered a Francophone author of the Maghreb. In Algeria, his legacy is complex. He is mostly remembered as the author of poems such as "Citizens of Beauty." But, his more erotic, intimate poetry has been marginalized.

After Sénac's death in 1973, the Moroccan author, Tahar Ben Jelloun, who had met Sénac in his youth, wrote: "I think of his furor, his cries, his refusals: because the Arab world that he loved has forgotten, in a particularly harsh way, what it knew of freedom and poetry, only to replace them with false-hoods backed up with arms and the gloved hand placed over the mouths of those who attempt to speak." Sénac, the *gaouri*, left behind a vast body of work, in which he elaborated his vision for what he hoped could be the reconciliation between European and Islamic cultures, and for an Algeria of openness and plurality.

7 Boudjedra, 71,75

Poèmes

Poems

NOCES

Tout ici est de peau bronzée
abricot doux comme une fièvre
les regrets ont mis sur mes lèvres
la nourriture d'un été

Tout ici est d'algue rapide
caressante comme un secret
le corps étend sa vanité
sous une parole limpide

Tout ici est de sable exact
où le pied brouille les chemins
avant de retirer la main
tu refais ta mer excessive

Tout ici est d'amour fragile
à la mesure du soleil
tu déniches dans un orteil
lancinant le dépôt des îles

Tout ici est d'haleine vive
de prouesses désordonnées
le rire souple des pagaies
renoue les foires primitives

Tout ici est suant de sève
son corps têtu comme ses mots
sa voix charnue comme son rêve
son cœur tendu entre deux eaux

Tout ici installe la gloire
l'orgueil aliène la raison

NOCES

Here everything is sun-baked skin
apricot sweet as a fever
regrets have placed upon my lips
the sustenance of summer

Here everything is swift seaweed
affectionate as secrecy
the flesh extends its vanity
beneath a limpid word.

Here everything is accurate sand
that the foot kicks up across the paths
and then when you withdraw your hand
you recreate your extravagant sea

Here everything is fragile love
made to the sun's dimension
and you unearth with a throbbing toe
the islands' vast deposits

Here everything is intense breath
disorderly exploits
the supple laugh of dipping oars
revives the primitive fairs

Here everything is sweating sap
his body stubborn as his words
his voice as carnal as his dream
heart stretched between two pools

Here everything's made glorious
pride abandons reason

Quelle joie trouble la saison
et réussit à l'émouvoir?

Castiglione, 22 juillet 1949

What joy disturbs the season
and successfully arouses it?

Castiglione, July 22, 1949

CAP CAXINE

La courbe de la crique
à ta jambe nerveuse

Le gisant de la roche
à ta lèvre étonnée

L'impudeur de la vague
à ton œil indécis

L'inceste du soleil
à ton sein refusé

Le regret de l'éponge
au labyrinthe ému

Je m'use à te convaincre
une caresse sotte
essaie de desceller
la pierre des genoux

Toute une vie à défendre
tout un amour à reprendre
un désert à flamme fendre

Mai toi
je t'appelais
la nuit couvrit ma voix.

Alger, 10 octobre 1949

CAPE CAXINE

The curve of the rocky beach
to your nervous leg

The recumbent figure of the rock
to your astonished lip

The shamelessness of the wave
to your uncertain eye

The incest of the sun
to your rejected breast

The regret of the sponge
to the agitated maze

I wear myself out convincing you
a foolish caress
tries to loosen
the stone from between your knees

An entire life to defend
an entire love to start again
a desert in flames for me to transcend

May
I called you
The night concealed my voice.

Algiers, October 10th, 1949

9

LANGAGE

Entre ces choses dures
qui s'exaltent de la mort à la vie
et des lèvres aux plaies
il y a le mutisme sûr
qui seul assure l'homme exact
il y a le silence pétillant fidèle
plus tendre que les mots sans voix
il y a une heure capable
d'aube immobile et de pied nu

Quand je dois trouer cette larme
figée absente au corps
qui demeure plus haut que rêve
et nie le cours de la saison
quand je dois brouiller ma présence
et pur donner ma langue à tous
je parle sans penser des objets que je vois

Je dis que le rideau se rouille sous la vitre
je dis que la mie sèche sur la table accablée
je dis que le baigneur lègue un corps désirable
je dis que la mer est aussi bleue que les blés
je dis que le vin chante au menton mal rasé
je dis que la serviette a l'odeur de tes songes
je dis que les souliers sont la courbe du monde
je dis que ton doigt germe autant que les genêts

Tu me regardes
ému.
tu cherches une source
tu sépares le bain de l'eau

LANGUAGE

Between these difficult things
flared up from death to life
from lips to wounds
there is a sure silence
that alone reassures the man of precision
a sparkling faithful silence
more tender than those voiceless words
an hour capable
of an immobile dawn and bare feet

When I must pierce that tear
suspended absent from the body
remaining higher than a dream
and denying the course of the seasons
when I must cloak my presence
and pure give my language to everyone
I speak without thinking of the things that I see

I say that the curtain rusts below the window
I say that the bread grows stale on the unstable table
I say that the bather bequeaths his delectable body
I say that the sea is as blue as wheat
I say that the wine sings to the scruffy chin
I say that the towel is scented with your thoughts
I say that the shoes are the curve of the earth
I say that your finger springs up as thick as broom

You look at me
moved
you search for a source
you separate the bath from the water

Et je mens juste pour t'aimer

Ma vérité n'a pas de bornes
elle boite pour s'assurer
que sa démarche reste vive

Tu rêves confondu par un si pur mensonge
je te comprends je prends ta main

Si le mot était de pain
il passerait mieux la gorge
nous pourrions enfin être heureux.

Alger, 12 août 1949

12

And I lie just to love you

My truth has no limits
it limps to reassure itself
that it retains a lively step

You dream confused by so pure a lie
I understand you I take your hand

If the word were bread
it would go down more smoothly
and we could be happy at last.

Algiers, August 12, 1949

Matinale de mon peuple

*Ces textes ne veulent être que des documents lyriques au fronton
d'une lutte. Puissent des matins justes les effacer demain.*

J.S.
Alger–Oran, novembre 1949
Paris, novembre 1957

My People's Early Rising

These texts aspire only to be lyrical documents engraved on the pediment of a struggle. May just dawns erase them tomorrow.

J.S
Algiers-Oran, November 1949
Paris, November 1957

MATINALE DE MON PEUPLE
pour Baya

Tu disais des choses faciles
travailleuse du matin
la forêt poussait dans ta voix
des arbres si profonds que le cœur s'y déchire
et connaît le poids du chant
la tiédeur d'une clairière
pour l'homme droit qui revendique
un mot de paix
un mot à notre dimension

Tu tirais de sa solitude
le rôdeur qui te suit tout pétri de son ombre
celui qui voudrait écrire comme tu vois
comme tu tisses comme tu chantes
apporter aux autres le blé
le lait de chèvre la semoule
et si dru dans le cœur et si fort dans le sang
la bonté de chacun
le charme impétueux des hommes solidaires

Parle ô tranquille fleur tisseuse des promesses
prélude au sûr éveil de l'orge
dis que bientôt l'acier refusera la gorge
bientôt le douar entamera la nuit
Tu m'apprends à penser
à vivre comme tu es
Matinale arrachée à l'obscure demeure.

Alger, 1949

16

MY PEOPLE'S EARLY RISING
for Baya

You were saying easy things
hard-working woman of the morning
the forest grew in your voice
its trees so thick that hearts torn apart
know the full weight of song
the warmth of a clearing
for the upright man who demands
a word of peace
a word of human proportions

You pulled from his solitude the stalker
who steeped in shadows kept you in his sight
the one who wants to write the way you see
the way you sing, the way you weave
and bring the others wheat
goat's milk semolina
and thick in the heart and strong in the blood
the kindness of everyone
and the impetuous charm of men in solidarity.

Speak oh tranquil flower weaver of hope
prelude to the barley's certain awakening
say that soon steel will spurn the throat
that soon the douar will deal a blow to the night
You teach me to think
to live as you live
Torn from the dark abode, your early rising.

Algiers, 1949

17

LA PATRIE

Encore une fois, et pour une interminable présence, me voici au cœur de ma ville, cerné par mon peuple ouvrier. Je ne sais quel courant m'entraîne, ni quelle voix se fait entendre qui me conduit toujours vers le même refuge : la cour mauresque d'un ami, les blocs du môle où règne une jeunesse pauvre, affamée et joyeuse. Ces fières épaules que le bâton ni l'insulte n'ont courbées, près d'elles c'est bien ma force que je retrouve, notre avenir en grandes lettres solaires. Et je répète un nom, toujours le même, celui qu'aucune humiliation, aucune colère n'efface, le tien, Mère Algérie, notre inlassable amour.

Ici le café est bon. Et il est bon marché. Les assiettes sont grasses et la cuisine rouge. Le piment met du feu jusque dans nos propos. Est-ce le secret de cette langue, caillouteuse et roulant pépites dans la vase? J'aimerais dire ma certitude, mais au creux de ma joie une angoisse, un vieux remords veillent. Mes pères ont imposé à ce rivage une civilisation de maîtres, privée de son honneur et de ses vrais prestiges. Etaient-ils à ce point aveugles et incultes? Comme je me sens peu de leur race! Ces visages qui crient par leur seule présence et leur mâle douleur, ils ont cru les fermer! Que n'ont-ils médité l'aveu du conquérant: «Ce que j'admire le plus au monde, c'est l'impuissance de la force à fonder quelque chose.» Par eux, nous avons vécu sur cette terre en aventuriers nostalgiques, séquestrés par l'exil. Nous avons défini une «supériorité» hypocrite, mais la Vertu, grave et brûlante, se réfugiait derrière un treillis ou un voile, ou dans la conque des mosquées. Notre «blanc» n'était qu'une bonneterie de parvenus. Parvenus à quoi, je vous le demande? Nous avons grandi citoyens de patries étrangères quand la nôtre en Islam nous l'abandonnions à ses plaintes. A ses rêves grandioses. Nous avons péché par absence. Nous avons nié le soleil. Et notre patrie, sans nous, s'est écorchée la

HOMELAND

Once again, and as an unending presence, I am here in the heart of my city, surrounded by the working class. Some sort of current carries me along, some sort of voice makes itself heard, which leads me always towards the same refuge: a friend's Moorish courtyard, the stone blocks of the Mole where famished and joyful, the poor youths rule. Near those proud shoulders bent by neither the stick nor insults, I find my very strength again, our future writ large in solar letters. And I repeat a name, always the same, the one that no humiliation, no fit of anger erases, yours, Mother Algeria, our untiring love.

Here the coffee is good. And cheap. The plates are greasy and the food red. Pepper sets fire to our very words. Is that the secret of this language, stony and rolling, like golden nuggets in the mud? I would like to assert my certainty, but in the pit of my joy, anxiety and an old regret keep watch. My forefathers imposed on these shores a master civilization, with no honor and without its true importance. Were they really so very blind and uncultivated? How little I feel that I am of their breed! They thought that those faces, whose very presence and virile pain scream out, were impenetrable! But how they have reflected on the conqueror's confession: "What I admire most in the world, is that strength is powerless to establish anything." Because of them we have lived on this land as nostalgic rogues illegally confined by exile. We defined a hypocritical "superiority," while Virtue, serious and ardent, was taking refuge behind a uniform, a veil, or the shell of mosques. Our "white" was no more than a knitwear industry run by parvenus. Parvenus who succeeded at what, I ask you? We grew up as citizens of foreign lands whereas our own land was abandoned to Islam and its complaints. To its grandiose dreams. Our sin was having been absent. We

gorge, et son poing le voici qui martèle nos cœurs. Ô mes pères, pour nous qui avons pris racine dans ce peuple, comme vous vous trompiez, comme vous nous avez fait du mal ! Mais rien ne prévaut jamais contre l'Amour. Rien ne prévaut contre l'Espérance. Dans vos traditions reniées, nous avons saisi au vol quelques silex et des flammes têtues. Aux lisières de votre insolence, avec nos frères, nous avons élevé quelques broussailles vigilantes.

Dans les rues étroites, une voix fabuleuse de sables et de fer me lie à cette langue que je ne parle pas encore. Et pourtant, dans mon sang, c'est elle qui laboure, venue des lointaines Espagnes, et déjà me confie les noms terribles de l'hiver et la fraîcheur de la moisson.

Mon peuple m'entoure et murmure. Il prépare un réveil au relais de ses monts. Nous portons ensemble les stigmates. Qu'importe maintenant la haine ou l'indifférence de mes pères, puisque voici la vérité en route et que je marche dans ses rangs. Les enfants de Cortez seront toujours suspects? Qu'en savons-nous? Ce dont je suis assuré, c'est qu'une patrie se forge et se mérite.

Dans le crépuscule rouge et sombre, mon ami chante:

Nous sommes venus au monde fraternels!
Brisées soient les mains de tout Diviseur!

Je suis conscient de participer, d'échapper au singulier, de me sentir avec ceux que j'aime, non plus un rêveur déraciné mais un homme lucide. Et c'est pourquoi je sais que nous avons raison.

Alger, mars 1954
Paris, juillet 1955

20

repudiated the sun. And our homeland, without us, grazed its throat, and now its fist hammers away at our hearts. Oh, my forefathers, how you were mistaken, how you harmed those of us who have taken root among this people! But nothing ever overcomes Love. Nothing overcomes Hope. In your repudiated traditions, we have seized in mid-air flint stone and stubborn flames. At the border of your arrogance, we have planted some vigilant undergrowth.

In the narrow streets, a fabulous voice of sand and iron connects me to this language I don't yet speak. And yet, in my blood, this language having come from faraway Spain ploughs on, and already it entrusts me with the horrific names of winter and the coolness of harvest time.

My people surround me and murmur. They are preparing an awakening, relaying the mountains. Together we carry stigmata. What does the hatred or indifference of my forefathers matter now, since truth is moving forward and I march in its ranks. Will the children of Cortez always be under suspicion? What do we know? What I am sure of is that a homeland is being built and must be deserved.

In the red and dark twilight, my friend sings:

We came into the world as brothers!
May the hands of those who divide us be crushed!

I am aware that I am participating, that I am escaping the singular, that I feel that I am with those I love, no more a rootless dreamer but a lucid man. And that is why I know we are right.

Algiers, March 1954
Paris, July 1955

SALUT AUX ÉCRIVAINS ET ARTISTES NOIRS

Nous, Ecrivains Algériens,
saluons le Premier Congrès Mondial
des Ecrivains et Artistes Noirs,
par le cri de nos fusilles,
la douleur de nos femmes
et ce crime:
l'amertume de nos enfants.

Les saluons par tout le sang
de notre peuple sur nos phrases,
par tout le noir de notre peuple
sur nos mains de givre fou,
les saluons par l'espérance
de nos morts et de nos vivants,
par la misère souriante,
par la dignité patiente,
par la rage des prisons,
les saluons par l'avenir,
par cette fleur inaltérable
qui monte des corps mitraillés,
de nos étudiants trépanés,
de nos villages bombardés.

Les saluons par la réponse
de notre peuple à l'ignorance,
par les mains déchirées des femmes de ménage,
par le poing du Rebelle au bivouac des larmes
qui ranime l'amour.

O frères ! si notre syntaxe elle-même
n'est pas un rouage de la liberté,
si nos livres doivent encore peser

SALUTE TO BLACK WRITERS AND ARTISTS

We, Algerian Writers
salute the First World Congress
of Black Writers and Artists,[1]
with the cry of our executed,
the pain of our women
and this crime:
the bitterness of our children.

We salute them with all the blood
of our people on our phrases,
with all the grime of our people
on our hands of mad frost,
salute them with the hope
of our dead and our living,
with poverty smiling,
with dignity patient,
with prisons enraged,
salute them with the future,
with this steadfast flower
that climbs the bodies shot down
of our bullet-ridden young
from our bombed out towns.

Salute them with our people's
response to ignorance,
with the torn hands of cleaning women,
with the Rebel's fist giving new life to love
 in the bivouac of tears.

Oh, brothers! if our syntax itself
be not a cog of liberty,
if our books continue to weigh

1 The First International Congress of Black Writers and Artists was held in Paris in 1956.

sur l'épaule du docker,
si notre voix n'est pas un relais d'étoiles
pour le chemineau et pour le berger,
si nos poèmes ne sont pas eux aussi des armes de justice
dans les mains de notre peuple,
oh, taisons-nous!
  Frères Noirs, les Ecrivains Algériens,
s'ils osent élever la voix tandis que leurs frères tombent,
c'est pour vous transmettre le relais de leur Espérance,
cette flûte de nos montagnes
où la Liberté s'engouffre,
s'unit au souffle de l'homme
et chante!

Paris, le 22 septembre 1956

on the shoulder of the docker,
if for the rail worker and for the shepherd
our voice be not a shift work of stars,
if our very poems be not also weapons of justice
in the hands of our people,
oh, let us fall silent!
 Black Brothers, if we Algerian Writers,
dare raise our voices when our brothers are falling,
it is to relay to you their Hope,
that flute from our mountains
where Liberty blows,
unites with man's breath,
and sings!

Paris, September 22, 1956

ALGER AU LOIN
(GRAVÉ SUR L'HERBE)

à Jean Subervie, Abdelkader Kâlache,
Jean Digot et Jacques Miel.

Ici commence, dans une halte de verdure, à mi-chemin entre l'orage et le sourire de l'accueil, ici commence ma lumière, avec la compassion, et peut-être la mort.

O frères ! avant l'heure de choc, et tandis que dans l'ombre les taurillons affûtent notre éternité dissidente, ô frères, pardonnez ce répit, pardonnez la tiédeur odorante des feuilles.

Demain, la mer nous prend de face. Nous sommes aveugles de sable. La girelle dans notre sang, elle seule tient le soleil!

(O mon pays, voici le lien ! Cette eau sacrée qui vient du Môle, la vague torturée, l'énorme larme de colère, notre espérance ralliée!)

Je bois ces jours à gorge avide. Une dernière récompense au seuil acide de la nuit, parmi les purs déchets du cœur.

Atroce terre! Vie friande! Entre l'angoisse et la vertu, une minute encore, tandis qu'à mes lèvres de marbre mes lèvres de chiendent s'affrontent, une minute encore, dans l'eau glacée de La Loubière, se frayer une marelle de plaisirs! Une minute encore, dans les brindilles de Laguioule, allumer un feu qui ne consume pas, et dans le cœur aimé, nommer les choses les plus simples.

Recule, mort! Enraye dans ces pierres roses la marche abrupte du trident!

Et vous, mes lointaines familles, oh, ne ricanez pas des

FARAWAY ALGIERS
(CARVED IN THE GRASS)

> *to Jean Subervie, Abdelkader Kâlache,*
> *Jean Digot and Jacques Miel*

Here begins, in this resting place in the grass, mid-way
between the thunderstorm and the welcoming smile, here,
with compassion and perhaps death, begins my light.

Oh brothers! before the clash, and while the bull calves in
the shadows sharpen our dissident eternity, oh brothers, for-
give this respite, forgive the fragrant warmth of the leaves.

Tomorrow the sea will take us head on. The sand blinds us.
Only the rainbow wrasse in our blood can bear the sun!

(Oh, my country, here is the link! This sacred water that
comes from the Mole, the tortured wave, the enormous tear
of rage, our hope swelling!)

I drink in these days with a hungry throat. A final reward
on the caustic threshold of the night, among the heart's pure
refuse.

Foul land! Ravenous life! Between anguish and virtue,
while for one minute my marble lips confront my twitch
grass lips, for one more minute in the icy waters of La Lou-
bière, to clear a hopscotch of pleasures!   And one minute
more, to light a fire in the twigs of Laguioule that does not
consume, and name in the beloved heart the simplest things.

Death, retreat! Halt the trident's abrupt advance within the
rose-colored stones!

And you, my distant families, oh, don't snigger at the ex-

ramages de l'exile. Parmi tant d'inutiles phrases, un mot va demeurer, un geste, comme une note de guitare, où soudain mes écarts prendront allure de destin.

Je n'ai fait toute chose, je n'ai accompli de service, que pour toi seul, amour, lumière entre les hommes, fraternité!

Enfants de mon pays, je vous ai vus courir ensemble sur la plage, libérés de nos races et libérés du sang.

Enfants, pourrai-je voir votre bonheur adulte?

Recule, mort, recule et romps mes étriers!

Ici, dans la douce verdure, la nuit d'échardes me défend. La longue nuit sans qui le soleil est mirage.

Rodez, 8 septembre 1957

ile's warble. Among so many useless phrases, one word, one gesture will remain like a guitar note, where all at once my indiscretions will take on an air of destiny.

I did it all, I did my duty, for you alone, love, light between all men, brotherhood!

Children of my country, I saw you running on the beach together, freed from our race and freed from blood.

Children will I ever see your grown-up happiness?

Retreat, death, retreat and throw me from the saddle!

Here, in my sweet grass, I am defended by the splintered night. The long night without which the sun is a mirage.

Rodez, September 8, 1957

JEUNES GENS DE MON PAYS...

Jeunes gens de mon pays,
j'écris pour vous dans l'avenir,
vous qui viendrez libérés de la colère des ancêtres,
vous pour qui je ne serai plus l'oppresseur.

Vous ne fermerez pas la fontaine à ma soif,
ni jetterez à mon amour
l'os vigilant de vos charniers.
Malédiction bavarde ! Démagogies du Clan!
Que je me nomme Jean ne sera plus pour vous un signe
d'injustice.

Jeunes gens
un vieux monde en moi croule
et le grain se détruit.

Oh, j'appelle la nuit!
Que la nuit passe vite!
Au jour je vous salue.
Vous me reconnaissez.

30

YOUNG PEOPLE OF MY COUNTRY...

Young people of my country
I am writing for you in the future,
you who will arrive freed from the rage of your ancestors,
you for whom I will no longer be the oppressor.

You will not turn off the fountain to my thirst,
nor will you throw my love a vigilant bone from your
charnel houses.
Chattering Curse! Clan Demagoguery!
That my name is Jean will no longer be a sign of injustice
for you.

Young people
an old world is crumbling within me
and the seed is being destroyed.

Oh, I call the night!
May the night pass quickly!
In the daylight I salute you.
You will recognize me.

LES PORTEURS DE NOUVELLES

Qu'ils sont beaux les porteurs de nouvelles!
Ils diront : «Paix en Algérie!»
Nous saurons qu'Henri Alleg est libre,
Djamila Bouhired vivante!
(O lumière plus violente
que l'électrode des bourreaux,
que l'éclat des couperets à l'aube!)

Ils diront: «Ta mère sourit.
Dans ses cheveux la guerre a oublié ses cendres,
mais elle reprend plaisir aux ruses de son peigne!»

Et l'image de Ben M'hidi sera comme une pierre d'angle,
comme un ciment, cinq doigts contre l' erreur.

Nous saurons que le jour se lève
triomphalement,
et qu'un sang neuf se lève,
veines et pipelines,
pour animer le corps du peuple.

Qu'ils sont beaux les porteurs de nouvelles!
Qu'ils viennent pour l'émerveillement du cœur,
et qu'ils aillent répétant:
«Là était la ruine et là est le nid.»

THE BEARERS OF NEWS

How beautiful are the bearers of news!
They will say: "Peace in Algeria!"
And we'll know that Henri Alleg is free,
Djamila Bouhired alive!
(Oh light harsher
than the torturers' electrode
or the glare of blades at dawn!)

They will say: "Your mother is smiling.
The war forgot its ashes in her hair,
but she can once again take pleasure in the cunning of her comb!"

And the image of Ben M'Hidi will be as a cornerstone
like cement, five fingers against error.

We will know that the sun is rising in triumph,
that new blood is also rising,
veins and pipelines,
to revive the people's body.

How beautiful they are, the bearers of news!
May they come for the heart to marvel,
and leave repeating:
"Here was the ruin and now here is the nest."

Citoyens de beauté

Citizens of Beauty

CITOYENS DE BEAUTÉ

à Ahmed Hounaci

Et maintenant nous chanterons l'amour
Car il n'y a pas de Révolution sans Amour,
Il n'y a pas de matin sans sourire.
La beauté sur nos lèvres est un fruit continu.
Elle a ce goût précis des oursins que l'on cueille à l'aube
Et qu'on déguste alors que l'Oursin d'Or s'arrache aux
    brumes et sur les vagues module son chant.
Car tout est chant—hormis la mort!
Je t'aime!
Il faut chanter, Révolution, le corps sans fin renouvelé de la
    Femme,
La main de l'Ami,
Le galbe comme une écriture sur l'espace
De toutes ces passantes et de tous ces passants
Qui donnent à notre marche sa vraie lumière,
A notre cœur son élan.
O vous tous qui constituez la beauté sereine ou violente,
Corps purs dans l'alchimie inlassable de la Révolution,
Regards incorruptibles, baisers, désirs dans les tâtonnements
    de notre lutte,
Points d'appui, points réels pour ponctuer notre espérance,
O vous, frères et sœurs, citoyens de beauté, entrez dans le
    Poème!
Voici la mer. La baie (parce qu'elle est un fruit de la lumière
    et de notre regard).
Les jeunes corps sont pleins des signes de la mer.
(Oh je répète car la beauté sur notre page est d'une
    reconnaissance infinie...)
Tout est lumière et chant tandis que la Révolution façonne
    ses outils.
Voici la mer. Ton corps, marais salant où je règne assoiffé.
Nous boirons la mer. Je boirai ton âme.

CITIZENS OF BEAUTY
To Ahmed Hounaci

And now we will sing of love
For there is no Revolution without Love,
And no morning without smiles.
On our lips beauty is a relentless fruit.
It has that precise taste of sea urchins gathered at dawn,
The ones you savor as the Golden Urchin tears itself from
    the mist and its song modulates on the waves
For everything is song—except death!
I love you!
Sing, Revolution, of the Woman's body, endlessly renewed,
Of the Friend's hand,
Of the shapely curve, written across the void,
Belonging to all those who pass, man and woman,
Who provide our march its true light
And our heart its impetus.
Oh all of you who constitute serene or violent beauty,
Pure bodies in the tireless alchemy of the Revolution,
Incorruptible gaze, kisses and cravings as our struggle gropes
    along,
Pressure points, true points that punctuate our hopes,
Oh you, brothers and sisters, citizens of beauty, enter the
    Poem!
Here is the sea. The bay (because it is a fruit of light and of
    our gaze).
The young bodies abound with signs of the sea.
(Oh I repeat myself for the beauty that fills our page is
    infinitely grateful...)
While the Revolution forges its tools, everything is light and
    song.
Here is the sea. Your body, salt marshes where I reign in
    thirst.
We will drink the sea. I will drink your soul.

Ivre de sel. Ivre de soif. A petits coups je bois ton âme.
Quel espace dans nos connexions les plus closes !
Quelles mutilations dans cet alambic saccagé !
Tu rayonnes, porteuse de planètes,
Au bord des abîmes de lin.
Sur l'autre versant de nous-mêmes
Nous basculons. Voici la mer.

Voici les champs. Les sarments renfrognés. Mais les
     bourgeons, l'herbe parée, la terre
Large comme tes hanches! Et les palmes le long
Des larges routes goudronnées. Nous chanterons l'amour
Car la Révolution sur cette terre est l'élément de
     fécondation capitale.
Quelle gloire dans ce simple regard d'un enfant–sous ce voile
Quelle promesse! Que les matinées ici sont bouleversantes,
Perpétuellement neuves dans leurs modulations
—Qui chantera ici deux fois le même chant ?
Et maintenant l'amour à n'en plus pouvoir dire.
Sur nos dents éclatent les grenades nouvelles,
Les grenades de la conscience populaire, les fruits!
Ton corps était presque impalpable—et je le parcourais de
     mes lèvres!—mais presque,
Si grande était sur toi la multitude du soleil
Et le sable alentour.
(Les mots, dis-moi ô mon amour, les mots nous allons les
     remettre à neuf,
Les tirer à quatre épingles—qu'ils n'aient plus honte dans la
     gangue où le malheur les avait mis—
Qu'ils sortent, qu'ils aillent dans la rue, sur le Môle, dans les
     champs.
Comme toi, qu'ils aient le sourire apaisé. Dans
La bouche des mots l'épaisseur de la mer, l'épaisseur de tes
     lèvres!)
La beauté sur tes lèvres est un feu continu,

Drunk on salt. Drunk on thirst. Slowly I sip your soul.
What room there is in our most tightly sealed connections!
What mutilation in this ravaged alembic!
You are radiant, bearer of planets,
Teetering on the abysses of linen.
On the other side of ourselves
We tumble down. Here is the sea.

Here are the fields. The sulking vine. But the buds, the
    grass in its finery, the earth
As wide as your hips! The palms trees along
Wide tarred roads. We will sing of love
Because on this earth Revolution is the fundamental
    element of fertilization.
What glory in this child's simple gaze–beneath this veil
What promise! How deeply moving are the mornings here,
Ceaselessly new in their modulations
—Who among us will sing the same song twice?
And now with more love than can be expressed.
Across our teeth the new grenades explode,
The grenades of popular consciousness, the fruits!
Your body was almost intangible, almost—and I ran my lips
    over it!—
Because the multiple sun bore down so hard on you
And on the surrounding sand.
(Tell me my love, words, once more we will make words
    new,
Dress them to the nines—so that they're no longer ashamed
    of the restraints in which misfortune has placed them—
Let them go out, walk down the street, on the Mole, in the
    fields.
Let them go like you with a peaceful smile.
The words in your mouth as thick as the sea, as thick as your
    lips!)
Beauty on your lips is a relentless flame,

L'oiseau du soleil qui s'acharne dans sa ponte miraculeuse
—Et réussit!
O je n'en finis plus de saluer le jour, de mettre mon délire
Dans l'ordre quotidien, et sur ton corps
De l'ordonner, de donner vie à l'alphabet du rêve!
Je t'aime. La Révolution monte
Parmi la pure symphonie des jeunes corps face à la mer.

Et nous nous sommes approchés. Quel émerveillement, terre
    loyale,
Quelle bonté!
La beauté était là, pour le premier venu, à la portée de la
    main,
Vulnérable et farouche, un fruit en équilibre
Entre le regard et la faim. En moi
Des oiseaux, des oiseaux
Battaient, les mots prenaient
Leurs sandales de marche. Révolution,
Que la matinée était belle!
J'ai vu le peuple le plus beau de la terre
Sourire au fruit et le fruit se donner.

Car le fruit, si tu le convies aux fêtes de l'homme,
Il accourt.
Il éclate comme une pupille.
Tu crois qu'il est dans le désordre, il nage à brasses
    ordonnées.
Ecoute l'oursin la méduse
Qui se déploient pour se défendre:
Une mélodie de l'espace—et le cosmonaute répond.
Ton cœur n'éclate pas de joie, il s'arrondit, il se compose.
La paix est douce sur notre peau...

Je t'aime. Tu es forte comme un comité de gestion
         Comme une coopérative agricole

The sun bird struggles to lay its miraculous eggs.
—And succeeds!
Oh, I don't stop saluting the dawn, placing my delirium
In everyday order and arranging it
Across your body that I may bring to life the alphabet of
    dreams!
I love you. The Revolution rises
Through the pure symphony of young bodies facing the sea.

And we approached each other. What wonder, faithful land,
What kindness!
Beauty was there for the taking, close at hand,
Vulnerable and unflinching, a fruit striking the balance
Between gazing and hunger. Within me
Birds, birds
Beat, words seized
Their walking sandals. Revolution,
How beautiful was the morning!
I saw the most beautiful people on earth
Smile at the fruit, and the fruit give itself up to them.

For the fruit, if invited to man's celebrations,
Comes running.
It explodes like the pupil of an eye.
You think that it is in chaos, but it swims a meticulous
    breaststroke.
Listen to the urchin and the medusa
Deployed out of self-defense:
A melody from outer space—and the cosmonaut answers.
Your heart doesn't burst with joy, it gets rounder, more
    composed.
Peace is soft against our skin . . .

I love you. You are strong like a management committee
Like a farmer's cooperative

Comme une brasserie nationalisée
Comme la rose de midi
Comme l'unité du peuple
Comme une cellule d'alphabétisation
Comme un centre professionnel
Comme une parole de meddah
Comme l'odeur du jasmin dans la rue de
Tayeb
Comme une gouache de Benanteur
Comme le chant des murs et la métamorphose des slogans
Comme la soléa de ma mère
Les bleus les bruns de Zérarti
Comme les baigneurs à la Pointe-Pescade
Comme le Nègre de Timgad
La Vénus de Cherchell
Mon cœur mon graffiti.
Je t'aime. Tu es ma folie positive.
Comme une pastèque bien rouge
Comme le sourire d'Ahmed
Comme une chemise de Chine
Une djebbah de Yasmina
Comme un beau discours politique
Comme un camion plein de rires
Comme une jeune fille qui retire son voile
Comme une autre qui le remet
Comme un boucher qui affiche des prix bas
Comme un spectacle réussi
Comme la foule qui acclame
Comme Jean qui sur une pierre
Pose une autre et nomme la terre
Comme le jet d'eau dans la cour
Comme à la nuit la bouqala
Comme une prière de Djelal
Une élégie d'Anna Gréki
Comme une formule mathématique

Like a nationalized brewery
    Like the rose at noon
    Like the unity of the people
Like a literacy program
Like a training center
Like a meddah's word
Like the smell of jasmine on Tayeb's street
   Like a gouache by Benanteur
Like the song of the walls and the metamorphoses of slogans
Like my mother's solea
Zérarti's blues and browns
Like the beach-goers at Pointe-Pescade
Like Timgad's Blackman
Cherchell's Venus
My heart my graffiti.

I love you. You are my constructive madness.
Like a bright red watermelon
Like Ahmed's smile
Like a shirt from China
A djibbah from Yasmina
    Like a fine political speech
      Like a truck full of laughter
    Like a young girl removing her veil
Like another girl putting it back on
Like a butcher posting low-prices
Like a successful performance
Like the applauding crowd
Like Jean who puts down a rock
On the one where he's standing and names the land.
    Like the fountain in the courtyard
Like the nighttime bouqala
Like a prayer by Djelal
  An elegy by Anna Gréki
Like a mathematical formula

Comme l'histoire de Medjnoun
                        Et sa Leïla
Comme le défilé du 1er Novembre
                    Comme la certitude de Bachir
                    Comme les escaliers d'Odessa
            Comme à Tilioua les olives
Comme un danseur de hadaoui
                    Comme El Anka et sa colombe
Comme Yahia qui épluche le noûn
            Et comme Natalie qui épèle
Une orange.
Tu es ma poésie active. Je t'aime.
Oui tu es forte tu es belle
Comme les mots qui trouvent sur la feuille
            Notre douleur cicatrisée
            Notre miracle du pardon
                    Comme les youyous sur les terrasses
                            Le satellite qui répond
Comme un galet entre ta main
                    Et la mienne
Pour porter témoignage de l'été.
Ensemble nous avons affronté le ridicule,
Les habitudes acquises, les images courantes,
Les aciéries du capital.
Cet été les moissons furent bonnes.
La mer très bleue. Presque verte. Je t'aime.

Et maintenant pour nos enfants je dis la couleur de Tolga,
Ce bleu qui est venu frapper à notre vitre,
Pas le bleu de la mer mais un lit plus profond
Pour les loisirs simples de l'âme.
Et notre cœur, tout comme un drap, à ce bleu nous l'avons passé
(Regarde, il brille!)
Le sourire bleu de Tolga parmi ses ruines et ses palmes !
Et la dignité d'El Hamel!

44

Like the story of Mejnoun
And his Leïla
        Like the November 1st parade
Like Bachir's certainty
Like the Odessa stairs
  Like the olives of Tilioua
      Like a hadaoui dancer
Like El Anka and his dove
Like Yahia peeling the noûn
And like Natalie spelling out
an orange.
You are my active poetry. I love you.
Yes you are strong and beautiful
Like words that find their way to paper
Our pain healed over
Our miracle of forgiveness
Like the uluations on the terraces
The satellite that responds
Like a stone between your hand
And mine
To bear witness to the summer.
Together we face ridicule,
Habits deeply ingrained, routine images
And the steel mills of capital.
This summer the harvest was good.
The sea very blue. Almost green. I love you.

And now for our children I speak the color of Tolga,
That blue that came knocking at our window,
Not the sea's blue but a deeper bed
For the soul's simple leisure.
And like a sheet, we rinsed our heart in that blue.
(Look, it shines!)
The blue smile of Tolga among its ruins and palm trees!
The dignity of El Hamel!

M'Chounèche qui crépitait d'audace au fond des gorges!
Je n'en finirais plus de ranimer nos forges,
Je n'en finirais plus de nommer sur ton corps
Les infinis prolégomènes...
                              O Révolution patiente
Et têtue!
                    O ces dents qui sont la page blanche
Où mon poème se construit!
                              O nuit très douce
Dans les absinthes de tes bras!
Oui, n'aie pas peur, dis-leur
Que tu es belle comme un comité de gestion
                    Comme une coopérative agricole
                    Comme une mine nationalisée.
Osons, ô mon amour, parer de fleurs nouvelles
Le corps du poème nouveau!

Et même si l'horreur maintenant nous fait face
(Car rien n'est facile, non, et tout sans fin remis),
A la terrasse des cafés si nos singes bouffis
Grignotent l'avenir avec des cacahuètes
Et parlent de Ben M'Hidi comme d'un objet de
        consommation anodine
(O frère-dynamite ! O frère-flamme nue!
O frère-vent actif qui déracine la gangrène!)
Même si le découragement et la dérision nous assaillent,
Maintenant nous savons que nous sommes sauvés
Dans le grand geste socialiste
Car la Révolution et l'Amour ont renouvelé notre chair
(Salves ! Salves cent fois de tzaghrit et de graines!)
Je t'aime. Vers la mer
Les enfants de l'alphabet dressent leur joie comme des roseaux.
A l'ombre nous nous asseyons
Et tu t'émerveilles
Parce qu'une bête à bon Dieu vient se poser sur mon genou.

M'Chounèche, crackled with daring, deep inside the gorges!
I'll never see the end of re-stoking our forges,
I'll never see the end of naming, on your body,
An infinity of prolegomena. . .
Oh Revolution, patient
And stubborn!
Oh those teeth those white pages
On which the poem is being built!
Oh gentlest of nights
In the absinthes of your arms!
Yes, don't be afraid, tell them
You are beautiful as a workers' management committee
As a farmers' cooperative
A nationalized mine.
Let's dare, oh my love, to dress with new flowers
The body of the new poem!

And even if horror now faces us
(For nothing is easy, no, everything's indefinitely postponed),
If at café terraces our bloated bosses
Nibble on the future along with the peanuts
And speak of Ben M'Hidi as if he were a meaningless
    consumer good.
(Oh brother-dynamite! Oh brother-naked flame! Oh
    brother-vital wind that uproots gangrene!)
Even if discouragement and mockery assail us,
Now we know that we are saved
In the grand socialist gesture
For Revolution and Love have renewed our flesh
(Salvos! A hundred times salvos of ululation and seed!)
I love you. The alphabet's children
Lift their joy like reeds towards the sea.
We sit in the shade
And you marvel
Because a ladybug has landed on my knee.

Oui, ceux qui ont péri ne nous ont pas trompés.
C'est pourquoi maintenant nous chanterons l'amour.

Alger, janvier 1963
Pointe-Pescade, octobre 1963

Yes, those who have died did not betray us.
And this is why we now will sing of love.

Algiers, January 1963
Pointe-Pescade, October 1963

ARBATACHE
à Kayasse

1

Ce soir tu t'approches de moi plus confiant que d'habitude.
Tu as planté ton arbre.
Dans les youyous dans la sueur dans les sourires la parcelle
S'est repeuplée.
Les crispations d'hier n'ont plus de sens,
Ni ces nerfs que l'on nous arrache
Un à un.
Nous dirons L'Arbatache comme on dit
La Soummam ou La Sierra Maestra
Comme on dit Odessa ou La Commune de Paris
Comme on dit tu es belle tu grandis tu as fait des progrès tu
    sais lire.
Vert est notre drapeau : la foule qui reboise
Et le cœur qui bondit vers la mer au mois d'août.
Tant de nuits sont passées et tant de nuit nous ronge :
C'était la terre qui fout le camp.
Aujourd'hui tu répètes: «Regarde, Yahia, nous avons retenu
    la terre, nous avons retenu la vie.»
Où est le poème à cette heure
Sinon dans la main qui se dresse pour affirmer notre
    moisson,
Sinon sur tes lèvres où déjà
L'arbre a fructifié et l'oiseau
Ramené une part de ciel?
Je rêve nous rêvons
                    Au rythme des camions qui passent.
Et je t'embrasse, mon enfant,
Plus confiant ce soir d'avoir planté ton arbre.

50

ARBATACHE[1]

to Kayasse

1

Tonight you come to me more confident than usual.
You have planted your tree.
Through ululations, sweat, and smiles the plot of land
Has come back to life
Yesterday's tensions no longer hold any meaning,
Nor do the nerves that one by one
They are ripping out of us.
We'll say Arbatache as we do
Soummam or Sierra Maestra
As we say Odessa or the Paris Commune
As we say you are beautiful you've grown you've made
    progress you can read.
Green is our flag: the crowd that reforests
And the heart that in August bounds towards the sea.
So many nights have passed and so many more gnaw away at
    us:
It was the land that was making its escape.
Today you repeat: "Look, Yahia, we have held onto the land,
    we have held on to life."
Where is the poem at this moment
If not in the hand raised to bear witness to our harvest,
If not on your lips where already
The tree bears fruit and the bird
Has brought back a piece of sky?
I dream we are dreaming
To the beat of passing trucks.
And I kiss you my child,
Who tonight, having planted your tree, are more confident
    than ever.

---

1 A city in Algeria, formerly known as Maréchal-Foch, 34 kilometers from
Algiers, where in 1963 there was a large-scale reforestation campaign.

2

Puis il s'enfonce dans l'opaque.
Mon ombre est mauvaise, pensa-t-il,
Je suis un arbre à taches,
Un fouillis de nervures où les oiseaux s'enivrent
Et tombent dans la boue les plumes arrachées.
C'était un cauchemar d'automne.
La foule intacte autour de lui bâtissait une digue
Contre la mort.
Suis-je un passant d'un autre monde?
Un résidu de tant d'erreurs?
A nouveau l'Enfant sauta sur son cœur:
J'ai planté mon arbre !

3

Il sut que la Révolution
Fait d'une bavure une brique
D'une cendre un moellon.

Il sut que la nuit est courte
Malgré les heures longues longues
Pour qui place un soleil aux angles du logis.

Il sut que la confiance de l'Enfant
Est plus fertile que nos drames
Et domine nos déraisons.

Il sut que notre chair
Habile à se corrompre
Est prompte à récupérer son éclat.

Un jour nos montagnes reverdiront.

And then he disappears into the pitch-dark
My shade is offensive, he thinks
I am a tree of stains,
A bundle of veins where the birds get drunk
And fall in the mud with their feathers torn out.
It was an autumn nightmare.
The undiminished crowd around him built a bulwark
Against death.
Am I a passer-by from another world?
The dregs of so many errors?
Once again the Child sprung upon his heart:
"I have planted my tree!"

3

He learned that the Revolution
Turns blunder into brick
ashes into ashlar.

He learned that for those who place suns at the pitch of rooftops
The night is short
Despite the long long hours.

He learned that the Child's trust
Is more productive than our tragedies
And overcomes our folly.

He learned that our flesh
So easily corrupted
Is quick to recover its radiance.

One day our mountains will become green again.

4

Mais le bonheur, lui, dans ce jour aride
Traverse notre corps et ne s'arrête pas.
La mer peut venir battre et nos vertèbres
S'ouvrir à une effusion infinie,
Tout autour il n'y a que lassitude et désarroi.
A se demander même si l'amitié, l'amour poussent sur cette
terre,
Seulement avide de pain, de justice et d'une jouissance
impétueuse comme l'oubli.
La cavale ennemie—son luxe !—nous a si longtemps martelés
Et la vigne à ce cœur agrafé ses tessons
Qu'il n'y a plus de place pour une parole d'accueil
Ni pour une fleur aux fenêtres.
Regarde ces montagnes : pas une rose!
Pas une main de femme pour la rose!
Seulement la maigreur séculaire et les chiens qui aboient.

5

L'arbre et le pain, voilà ce qu'ils demandent.
Et dans la ville, un peu de joie,
Un peu de jouissances nocturnes : l'alcool, le twist après la
guerre!
Et sur les plaies encore ouvertes un peu de salive femelle.
Où est la rose? Où est l'arbre, le pain?
La parole dorée qui n'est pas une politesse, une écume?
Où est le respect? Où l'honneur?
Il passe sur ce pays un froid de nord extrême.

4

But happiness in this arid daylight
Passes straight through our bodies without stopping.
The sea can beat down, and our spines
Can open to the limitless outpouring,
Everywhere there is only weariness and utter confusion.
So much so that you wonder whether friendship and love
    grow on this land,
Which is only hungry for bread, for justice and pleasure that
    is as impulsive as oblivion
The enemy on the run—its riches!—pounded at us for so
    long
And the vine so fastened its sheath to that heart
That there's no room left for a word of welcome
Or a flower in the windows.
Look at those mountains: not a rose!
Not a woman's hand for the rose!
Only age-old frailty and barking dogs.

5

Trees and bread, here is what they are asking for.
And in the city a little joy,
A little night time pleasure: after the war, alcohol and the
    twist!
And on the still open wounds a little female spit.
Where is the rose? Where is the tree, the bread?
The golden word which is not frothy or insipid?
Where is respect? Where honor?
From the North a deep chill passes over this land.

6

Mais vient l'arbre. Il vient toujours même lorsque tu
    t'éloignes.
Il secoue ton vieux corps malade et tire son oiseau vers le
    ciel.
Entre la vigne et le charnier, il balbutie un mot
Qui conduit le soleil à tes lèvres, et tu chantes!
Arbatache, parce que la foule s'est levée!
Arbatache, parce que ton ombre est possible,
Même trouée, même noircie !
Arbatache, parce que nos larmes elles-mêmes
Vont irriguer le sol,
Même salées, même salies!
Arbatache, parce que la vie est plus forte
Dans le poing menu de l'Enfant
Que dans la main du bureaucrate!
Arbatache, parce que quatorze fois sur la route
Tu trébucheras et tu ramasseras ton outil!
Arbatache, parce qu'au bout de ta tristesse
Il y a un arbre planté!
Et demain la Rose!

La terre est friable, accueillante, mais ton âme est un roc
De solitude.
Les tzaghrit des femmes, les mains
Des gosses sur ton front
Ne sont que chariots qui passent,
Hirondelles d'exil.
C'est que la nuit a fait sa ponte avec splendeur,
C'est que les ténèbres sont riches,
Et tu gardes avec orgueil ce dur trésor. Combien de siècles
S'éparpillent dans tes vertèbres ?

6

But the tree comes. It always comes even as you retreat.
It shakes your old sick body and pushes its bird towards the
    sky.
Between the vine and the charnel house, it stammers a word
That leads the sun to your lips, and you sing!
Arbatache, because the crowd rose up!
Arbatache, because even when blackened and full of holes
Your shade is possible!
Arbatache, because our tears
Though salty and sullied
Will irrigate the soil!
Arbatache, because life is stronger
In the Child's slender fist
Than in the hand of a bureaucrat!
Arbatache, because on the road
You will stumble fourteen times and pick up your tool
Arbatache, because at the end of your sadness
A tree is planted!
And tomorrow the Rose!

7

The land is friable and welcoming, but your soul is a rock
Of solitude.
The women's ululations, the hands
Of kids on your brow
Are only passing carts,
Swallows of exile.
You see, night laid its clutch of eggs magnificently,
You see, darkness is fertile,
And proudly you guard this harsh treasure. How many centuries
Are strewn across your spine?
What diverted mountain streams carry to your heart

Quels torrents déviés charrient jusqu'à ton cœur
Le goût des morts? Car c'est la mort
Qui t'a pris par la taille, et danse, et tu le sais.
Reviens! Reviens vers nous ! Retiens la terre!
Retiens ce qui reste en toi de clarté!

8

Yé mmâ! Yé! comme un puits
Comblé d'orge putride je résonne.
Sur la margelle, à peine un peu de pluie.
Mais le soleil, la mer? C'était hier. Yé mmâ!
Je m'accroche à une herbe, à un sourire, au bruit
—Racines!—à quelque trace plus violente
Que ce cauchemar où je mords
La terre!
Yé mmâ, la terre ma complice
Et non l'éloge du bonheur!
Il faut du temps pour que la pioche
Arrive au cœur, fende le marbre,
Et que la graine s'épanouisse.
(Toi, dans ta ferme, tu le sais, mon fils!)
Du temps et pas toujours ce soleil qui rend fou!
Regarde, je t'appelle comme un enfant qui tète...
Yé mmaaaaaaaaaaaaaaaaaaaaaâ!

9

Un corps étreint n'est jamais une digue
Contre la nuit, mais au contraire
Un relais d'inquiétude qui brûle
Jusqu'au matin et te ramène au centre
Des douleurs. Si tu bâtis
Une citadelle de muscles
Le ver s'y met et tu titubes

The taste of corpses? For it is death
That took you by the waist, and dances and you know it.
Come back! Come back to us! Hold on to the land!
Hold on to whatever lucidity remains within you!

8

Yé mmâ! Yé! Like a well
Filled with rotting barley I echo.
On the edge of the well, just the slightest bit of rain.
But the sun, the sea? It was yesterday. Yé mmâ!
I cling to a blade of grass, to a smile, to a noise
—Roots!—to some traces more violent
Than this nightmare in which I bite into
The land!
Yé mmâ, the land is my accomplice
And not the glorification of happiness!
It takes time for the pickaxe
To strike the heart, to split open the marble,
And for the seed to bloom.
(You, on your farm, you know this, my son!)
Time and not always that maddening sun!
Look, I am calling you like a nursing child...
Yé mmaaaaaaaaaaaaaaaaaaaaâ!

9

A body locked in a tight embrace is never a bulwark
Holding back the night, no, it is
A relief from the worry that burns
Until morning and brings you back to the center
Of pain. If you build
A fortress of muscle
The maggots set in and you stagger
Drunk from the rot within.

Ivre de ton pourrissement.
Alors parfois la terre s'ouvre,
Tu y plonges, tu nages
Vers la racine, tu luttes
Encerclé de miroirs, tu gagnes
Un espace éveillé plus vaste que la mer.
C'est là que t'attendent les arbres
Que tu n'as pas plantés, les fruits béants, l'odeur
Des ténèbres anciennes. Tu mords le fruit
Fidèle à ton entêtement. Quelle fidélité
Dérisoire! La mort
Recommence son bal sur chaque corps étreint.

(Que cherches-tu depuis seize ans, quelle racine,
Ou quelle écharde dans ton corps à retirer?)

10

Si tu mords la terre, son goût
Tu le gardes toujours blotti dans une dent.
Tu as envie de crier: Ils sont tous pourris,
Laissez-moi écouter Rameau, El Anka, Djamila,
Laissez-moi écouter ma mère—ses rengaines de mauvais
    goût,
Laissez-moi me perdre dans ces dessins que les enfants
    tracent à la craie dans les rues de Pointe-Pescade,
Laissez-moi, laissez-moi—et pavoisez vos barques,
Empiffrez-vous dans les festins!
Que sont vos querelles, vos œuvres,
Quand mon peuple crève de faim?
O jeunes! ô lycéens, fellahs, chômeurs des villes et affamés
    des douars,
Levez-vous et dressez vos alphabets, votre culture orale
    contre leurs vers médiocres!
—Ces vers déjà qui rongent nos racines,

Then sometimes the earth opens up,
You dive in, you swim
Towards the root, you struggle
Surrounded by mirrors, you reach
A space stirred awake and vaster than the sea.
There the trees
You did not plant await you, their fruit bursting, and the scent
Of ancient darkness. You bite into this fruit
True to your stubborn nature. But what a pathetic
Truth it is! Death
Starts its dance again with every body locked in a tight embrace.

(What have you been searching for these sixteen years, what
    roots,
Or what splinter to be freed from your body?)

10

If you bite into the land,
Its taste stays in your mouth forever.
You feel like screaming: They are all rotten,
Let me listen to Rameau, El Anka, Djamila,
Let me listen to my mother—her same old vulgar tunes
Let me lose myself in those chalk drawings children scrawl
    on the streets of Pointe-Pescade,
Let me, let me—and string pennants across your boats,
Stuff yourselves at the feast!
What are your petty squabbles, your works of art,
When my people are starving?
Oh youth! Oh high-schoolers, fellahs, unemployed workers
    of the city and the hungry from the douars,
Rise up and set your alphabets, your oral culture up against
    their mediocre verse men!
Those vermin that are already gnawing at our roots,
But the roots can resist their nibbling.

Mais la racine est plus forte que leurs grignotements.
Alors, plutôt que le banquet,
Mords la terre et garde ce goût dans une dent
—La dent du pauvre: têtue, furieuse et bonne,
Dent d'amour et de bonne faim.

11

Car au-delà, prenant appui sur cette bouche, il y a toujours
le sourire de l'homme.
Celui qui cristallise l'espoir—l'Arabe
Pour affirmer une Arabie Heureuse!
Et ce sourire, s'il dialogue avec le peuple, pourquoi ne serait-
il pas la pierre la plus généreuse de notre république des
Pauvres?
Je vous le dis comme je l'ai senti dans la vaste respiration des
foules,
aussi sûr que la mer est bleue
et la terre rendue à ceux qui la cultivent.
«S'il fait bien son travail,
c'est bien ...»
«Un seul héros: le peuple»,
mais si le peuple a besoin d'un regard pour éclairer son
exigence,
s'il a besoin d'un nom, d'un visage, pour donner au
socialisme abstrait un contenu charnel,
alors n'ayons pas de ces retenues très intelligentes
et nous aussi intellectuels, prenons le souffle populaire
pour crier: Yahia Ben Bella ! Vive Ben Bella le pauvre!
«S'il fait bien son travail...»

So rather than a banquet
Take a bite of the land and hold its taste in your mouth
The hunger of the poor: stubborn, furious and good,
The hunger of love and the healthy appetite.

11[2]

Because, beyond that, if we rely on that mouth, at least there
    is always that man's smile.
The one who crystallizes hope—Arab hope
Who can deliver a Happy Arabia!
And, if it speaks to the people, why wouldn't that smile be
    the most generous stone in our Republic of the Poor?
I'm just telling you what I felt in the vast collective breath of
    the masses,
as sure as the sea is blue
and the land returned to those who cultivate it.
"If he does his work well,
it's good..."
"Only one hero: the people,"
but if the people need a countenance to shine on their
    demands,
if they need a name, a face, to give flesh to the abstractions
    of socialism,
then let's not show restraint in our highly clever manner
and we intellectuals, let us also join the exhalation of the
    multitudes and cry out:
"Yahia Ben Bella! Long live Ben Bella the poor man!"
"If he does his work well..."

2 This stanza did not appear in the first 1967 edition of the poem; in its place was
the word "Forthcoming." The section was removed after President Ahmed Ben
Bella was ousted by Colonel Houari Boumédiène in 1965, and the poem was only
published in its entirety posthumously.

«Mon peuple est aliéné, torturé, trépané,
Mon peuple est dans la souffrance et n'a pas de pain.»
Non, mon frère, ce ne sont plus les monstres colonialistes,
C'est le napalm de nos bourgeois, des profiteurs, des
  «militants» sans base
—Et ils n'y vont pas de main morte!
L'ennemi pour eux n'a pas changé:
C'est le patriote, le peuple.
Ils saboteront tout afin que rien ne bouge,
Masqués de surenchères, de lèches, de diplômes.
Les rues de nos villes, les ministères empestent, la lèpre s'abat
  sur nos douars!
Camarades, les ordures envahissent le sang!
Il y a corruption et crime!
Ministres-militants, frères à la base, frère-président, regardez-
  les qui bavent:
Le sang de Ben M'Hidi c'est leur coca-cola!
Ceux qui apprennent sont le peuple,
Ils ont leur place parmi nous;
Ceux qui n'ont rien appris sont les bourreaux du peuple.
Et les bourreaux ce soir pavanent dans les rues.
Alors?

Allons, éloigne-toi de toute cette aigreur.
Ecris et porte au peuple le meilleur de ton rythme
—Pas les faux pas, ni les courses d'envie,
L'Elan, lui seul (qui porte aux cimes).
La Révolution là-haut te fait signe : le sourire de Ben
  M'Hidi
—Et là-haut, c'est tout simple : au niveau de tes bras.
J'ai eu très mal tout un hiver, j'ai vu les meilleurs s'allier aux

"My people are crazy, tortured, lobotomized,
My people are suffering and have no bread."[3]
No, my brother, it isn't the colonial monsters anymore,
It is the napalm of our bourgeois, of our profiteers, of those
    rootless grassroots "militants"
— And they don't pull their punches!
For them the enemy hasn't changed:
It is the patriots, the people.
They will sabotage everything so that nothing changes,
Concealed by overblown promises, bootlickers, and diplomas.
The streets of our cities, the ministries reek, leprosy falls
    upon our douars!
Comrades, filth taints our blood!
All around us there is corruption and crime!
Militant-ministers, grassroots brothers, brother-president,
    look at them drool:
Ben M'Hidi's blood is their Coca-Cola!
Those who learn are of the people,
They have their place among us;
Those who have learned nothing are the torturers of the people.
And torturers are strutting in the streets tonight.
So?

13

Come, distance yourself from all this bitterness.
Write your finest measures and bring them to the people
— No missteps, no competitions of envy,
Momentum, alone (the kind that carries us to the mountain tops).
Up there the Revolution waves to you, Ben M'Hidi's smile

3 Sénac is quoting from his own poem from *My People's Early Rising* titled "My People Are Suffering."

médiocres—et braire!
J'ai collé sur la nuit des papillons tenaces.
Ma tête vrombissait des avions de Paris, de ceux de La
    Havane:
Fuir, fuir, oublier rien qu'un instant ce peuple!
«Tiens bon» répétait Mohamed qui construisait
    l'autogestion,
Et «Merci» ajoutait Kayasse.
Merci de quoi? Merci, à moi?
A toi!
J'étais dans le printemps une poignée de graines sans terre,
Une poignée de graines inutile
Face au grand schisme de ma voix.
Je me réfugiais dans mes draps—les plaintes de la mer me
    lacéraient les os.
Où étions-nous dans cet exil féroce?
Et toi, Révolution, dans quelle dent cachée?
J'interrogeais la nuit, j'interrogeais la foule,
Le sourire d'Ali, celui d'Abderrahmane,
Lumumba aux crachats, Yveton, Thuveny—mutants de
    l'esprit fou,
Je demandais à Khemisti : frère une fois de plus aide-moi,
Je téléphonais à Amar, à Bachir, à Robert, à Mourad, à Jean, à Djamal,
Je retrouvais mes murs, désemparé, lucide.
Mais où donc le soleil s'était mis cette fois?
Où est ma République des Pauvres?

14

Tu reviens. Tu as planté ton arbre.
Tu souris. Ton sourire a retenu la terre.
Enfant,

— And up there, it's quite simple: as far as your arms are
    concerned.
For an entire winter, I was in pain, I saw the best ally
    themselves with the mediocre—and bray!
I pinned stubborn butterflies to the dark.
My head throbbed from the planes in flight from Paris and
    Havana:
Escape, escape if for only a second forget this people!
"Hold tight" Mohamed, who was organizing self-
management, used to repeat,
And "Thanks" Kayasse would add.
Thanks for what? Thanks, to me?
To you!
In the spring I was a handful of landless seeds,
A handful of useless seeds
Confronted with my voice's great internal divisions.
I hid beneath my sheets—the sea's moans slashed my bones.
Where were we in this savage exile?
And you, Revolution, in whose mouth did you take refuge?
I questioned the night, I questioned the crowd,
Ali's smile, Abderrahmane's,
Lumumba as he was spit on, Yveton, Thuveny—mutants of
    mad hope,
I asked Khemisti: brother, help me once more,
I phoned Amar, Bachir, Robert, Mourad, Jean, Djamal,
I found my walls once again, at a loss, lucid.
But where has the sun placed itself this time?
Where is my Republic of the Poor?

14

You return. You have planted your tree.
You smile. Your smile has kept something of the land.
Child,
Cleanse me of death,

Lave-moi de la mort,

Lave-moi de la boue.

Je placerai mes vers sur tes lèvres et s'ils lèvent

Je saurai que mes jours ne sont plus un exil.

Car déjà sous les mots une tige s'élance.

Une tige! Et demain la Rose! Le Jardin! La Forêt!

Nous sommes seuls mais nous sommes solidaires.

Sommes-nous seuls?

Retiens la terre, Enfant, retiens-la dans mon cœur.

Les slogans ne suffisent plus

—Ils ne suffisent pas, mais chante,

Chante à n'en plus pouvoir et remplis notre corps de
    l'évidence des forets!—

Il faut la dure patience quotidienne

—Le cèdre, le caroubier—

Et plus haut que l'écœurement

—Le chêne, l'eucalyptus, l'olivier—

La force de croire au fruit malgré les branches mortes

—Le palmier, le pin, l'oranger, l'aloès et les mimosas—

Mortes, si elles l'étaient! mais non, viciées, arrogantes, agressives.

Il faut encore planter un arbre—un autre, un arbre propre

—Un pour chaque frère tué, pour chaque sœur.

C'est une longue marche, mon enfant—on nous mord les chevilles.

Le socialisme est une longue route et les brigands sans cesse
    affûtent l'ironie et les fils barbelés.

Mais il y a ton sourire, il y a l'Arbre—le bétoumier !

Il faut combattre, il faut marcher, combattre, retrouver le sens de 54.

Combattre et semer. Planter et protéger le plant.

Et défendre l'Arbre. Trouver le sens de 64.

La patience et la certitude ouvrières.

La joie à maintenir. Le chant.

Nous mettrons nos sandales de marche.

Nous progresserons vers l'Amour.

Nous progresserons vers la Rose !

Pointe-Pescade, 1er-24 décembre 1963

Cleanse me of mud.
I will place my poetry on your lips and if it comes alive
I'll know my days are no longer an exile.
For already beneath the words a stalk soars upwards.
A stalk! And tomorrow the Rose! The Garden! The Forest!
We are alone but we stand together.
Are we alone?
Take hold of the land, Child, take hold of it in my heart.
Slogans no longer are enough
— They're not enough, but sing,
Sing until you can't sing anymore and fill our bodies with
    the unmistakable essence of forests!—
You'll need a firm ordinary patience
— The cedar tree, the carob—
Ascending passed disgust
—The oak, the eucalyptus, the olive tree—
Then strength to believe there's fruit despite the dead branches
—The palm tree, the pine, the orange, aloe and mimosa—
If only they were dead! And not contaminated, arrogant, aggressive.
A tree—an unsullied tree—still needs to be planted
—One for every brother killed and every sister.
It's a long march, my child—they are snapping at our heels.
Socialism is a long road and the bandits unceasingly sharpen
    their irony and their razor wire.
But there is your smile, there is the Tree—the pistachio
We need to fight, march, fight, find once more the spirit of '54
Fight and sow. Plant and protect the seedling.
And defend the Tree. Find the spirit of '64.
Working class patience and certainty.
Joy must be sustained. The song.
We will put on our marching sandals.
We will make our way towards Love.
We'll make our way towards the Rose!

Pointe-Pescade December 1-24, 1963

CHANT FUNÈBRE POUR UN GAOURI

1

Jeunes gens ne demandez pas d'autographe au poète.
Il y a si longtemps que je n'écris plus au stylo mais à la
    bouche!
Mon soleil ? C'est le hérisson dans la vase dont on a tiré une
    à une toutes les pointes.
Je ne sais plus signer que d'un baiser avide.
Les mots dans mes doigts
               Saignent.
J'avance, les mains grand
Ouvertes.
Je n'écris plus, mes mains sont trop pleines de curieux.
Jadis mon corps était une volière
              Et le poème
Allait d'un groupe à l'autre
Porteur de pain, d'anis et d'oignon frais—la fête
Emplissait les terrasses. Ecoutez
L'élégie de Bartók où le jour et la fin
Des choses s'affrontent, s'amplifient. Nous voulions vivre.
J'ai mis mes sandales de mort.
Les fleurs
Ont mis des becs, les vagues des dentelles,
Mais rien n'a retenu le pèlerin vorace. Il mord
Pour avancer. Il meurt
Dans l'odeur de ses mots. Il porte
Le pli de l'horreur sur sa face. Le drap
Est tiré sur sa nuque où jadis le soleil...

2

« Jeunes gens, ne demandez pas d'autographe au poète.
Votre signature est plus ample,

DIRGE FOR A GAOURI[1]

1

Young people, don't ask for autographs from the poet.
For some time I have written not with a pen but with my
    mouth!
My sun? It is the muddy sea urchin whose needles have
    been plucked one by one.
I can sign my name now only with a hungry kiss
The words in my finger
Bleed.
I move forward, my hands wide
Open.
I no longer write, my hands are too full of witnesses.
Once long ago my body was a bird cage
And the poem
Flew from one gathering to another
Carrying bread, anise and fresh onions—celebration
Filled the café terraces. Listen
Bartók's Elegy where day and the end
Of things face off and grow more heated. We wanted to live.
I slip on my death sandals.
The flowers
Put on their quill points, the waves their lace,
But nothing held back the voracious pilgrim. He gnaws
His way forward. He dies
In the stench of his words. He wears
The wrinkle of horror on his face. The shroud
Is pulled over his nape, where long ago the sun....

2

"Young people, don't ask the poet for an autograph.
Your signature is freer,

1 A pejorative term for a foreigner meaning "infidel"

Fusée espiègle et grave du seul espace qui nous concerne
Où se love l'avenir
En toutes lettres—et l'aube sur vos dents!
Souriez sur le sable tandis que la mer nous parcourt,
Entraîne les détritus, force les grilles.
Je n'aurai pas de stylo dans la main,
Je la veux libre pour tracer notre joie,
Disponible pour s'unir aux vôtres.
L'après-midi avance ... »
                        Voila ce que jadis j'écrivais—et
Jadis c'est à peine un an !

                        3

Jeunes gens ne demandez rien mais donnez encore
Un sourire au poète. C'est la dernière écharde pour retenir
    son corps
Au bord de la falaise. La mer
Etait un lieu de joie, elle est
L'opaque où s'engloutit ce qui me reste d'âme. Je suis
Un tourbillon de négations et de désordre. J'écris
Avec mes ongles un poème sur vos
Pupilles, jeunes gens...La fin.

                        4

Je ne sais plus signer que d'un regard avide
Sur le sable tandis
Que vos muscles se tendent—la vie!
Et ma chair se défait ...
Les idées ne sont pas des barricades. Elles
Geignent sous la peau. Les adolescents sur
Le stade foulent le verbe et l'herbe
Envahit notre sang. C'était cela
La poésie, la gloire? O
Dérision !

A naughtier and more serious rocket to launch toward the
    only space we care about
Where the future is curled up
letter by letter–and the dawn is on your lips!
Smile on the sand while the sea moves over us
Carrying off the refuse, forcing open the gates.
I will not hold a pen
I want my hand free to trace our joy,
Ready to join with yours
The afternoon advances. . ."
                              This is what I wrote ages ago—and
Ages ago was barely last year!

3

Young people, ask for nothing but give
The poet one more smile. It is the last scrap propping his body up
At the cliff's edge. The sea
Had been a place of joy and is now
The darkness that drowns what's left of my soul. I am
A whirlwind of negations and confusion. With my nails
I scratch out a poem on your
Eyes, young people...The end.

4

I can sign my name now only with a hungry look
On the sand while
Your muscles become taut—life!
And my flesh comes undone...
Ideas are not barricades. They
Groan under the skin. Adolescents in
The stadium trample the word and the grass
And invade our blood. That was
Poetry, glory? Oh
Irony!

Je
Nie en moi ce je qui n'est que ma ténèbre.
Mes vertèbres se font
Liquide et vers la mer
S'écoulent. La mer!

Une confusion de rythmes envahit ma mémoire et
Brouille les racines. Où est
Le cœur? Je n'ai
Qu'un charroi de grelots. Je n'ai
Qu'une meute de guêpes à l'endroit où
L'organe chantait.
Je n'ai plus de sursaut, conscience, que l'orgasme. Où
Suis-je? en quel
Etat de veille? vers
Quelle autre misère accourant? La
Mort est le relais limpide. O
Phrases, arrachez à mon rêve encore un
Cri!

Afin que des enfants témoignent que je n'étais pas
    seulement un bidon
D'ordures.

Mais
Frappe
Encore

I
Deny in myself the I that is none other than my dark shadow.
My spine turns to
Water and flows to the sea.
The sea!

Confused rhythms invade my memory and
Obscure the roots. Where is
The heart? I have
Only a jangle of nerves. And
A pack of howling wasps where
My organ once sang.
No more jumping in alarm, no more consciousness only an
    orgasm. Where
Am I? in what
Wakened state? towards
What other hurried misery?
Death is the unimpeded relay. Oh
Sentences, rip from my dream one more
Scream!

So that children may testify I wasn't only a can
Of garbage.

But
Strike
Again

Toi
Soleil!
Dru
Sur
Mes os
        Vivants encore
Frappe!

9

Et n'arrête pas de saisir sur mes lèvres cette tendresse, toi qui
    la possédas un jour.

10

Néant. Mais si. ..
Non, seulement saccage
Tandis que le corps fuse
Vertigineusement vers la marée.
Poissons, filets, barques, rivage, c'est une imagerie
Pour tenir encore debout
Une saison. Mais l'âme
Ne tient plus le coup. Elle exige,
Arrogante, SA mort.

11

J'interroge.
Je me lève sur mon banc et j'appelle.
Pas d'autographe, jeunes gens, mais une place parmi vous
Pour croire qu'un matin peut encore paraître
Plus ferme que l'exil.

You
Sun!
Heavily
On
My bones
Still living
Strike!

9

And don't stop snatching from my lips that tenderness you
once possessed.

10

Nothingness. But if...
No, only havoc
While the body streams out
Vertiginously towards the tide.
Fish, nets, boats, shore, it's these images
That keeps you upright for another
Season. But the soul
Can't keep going on. It demands,
Arrogantly, ITS death.

11

I question.
I get up on my soapbox and call out.
No autographs, young people, just a place among you
To believe there'll come a morning still
More unyielding than exile.

12

Car c'est cela l'exil,
Sans fin, le lieu
Refusé. Peut-on vivre
Sans la patrie. Sans SA
Patrie au plus intact. Le corps
Est déchiqueté, délavé
(Vieux blue-jeans aux accrocs)
Quand lui est refusée sa terre,
Celle à lui
—Même terre de ronces,
Rocaille et rongements
Du sang, mais sienne!
(La terre qui est la forme immobile du peuple,
Sa densité la plus secrète - architecture et panoplie.)
Je me détruis comme celui
Qui aime sans réponse. La mer
N'est plus qu'un froid très âpre
Où se cognent mes jours. J'étais
Nu dans le verbe. Je suis
Une corbeille de loques qui
Roule vers l'abîme—et tant mieux
Si cette terre n'est pas à moi!

Je n'étais pas né pour ces plaintes ni pour que
La rose se brise à mon chant. L'éclat
Du jour je le portais au poing—faucon nubile de mes rêves.
Que de chasses—phrases levées! Quelles tonnes
D'étourneaux sur nos lèvres! Quelles nuits
Avec le rossignol comme un soleil de cendres!
Vivre avait ce goût sec des poissons que l'on mange
Sous les voûtes d'El Djezaïr, et la saveur des sauces

12

For that is exile,
Endless, the place
Denied. Is it possible to live
Without a homeland. Without ONE'S
Homeland in one piece. The body
Is ripped to shreds, faded
(Torn old blue jeans)
When his land is denied him,
His land
— Even a land of brambles,
Boulders and gnawing
At the heart. But still his!
(Land that is the unchanging shape of the people,
Its most secret density—architecture and armor.)
I am destroying myself like
An unrequited lover. The sea
Nothing now but a cold and very bitter place
Where my days get battered about. I used to be
Naked in the word. Today I am
A basket of rags
Rolling towards the abyss—And so much the better for it
If this land is not mine!

13

I was put on earth not to complain like this nor to
Shatter the roses with my song. On my fisted hand,
I carried the light of day—nubile falcon of my dreams.
How many Phrase-swatters held up! What bird-brained ideas
     fly from our lips! What evenings spent
With a nightingale like a sun of ash!
Living had that dry taste of fish eaten
Under the vaulted ceilings of El Djezaïr, and the flavor of sauce—

—Le laurier, le cumin, l'ail et la goutte d'ombre
Où mijote l'invention.
Je t'aime—mais quoi, je parle à vide!
J'ai laissé mon amour aux cigales d'Europe.
J'ai tout donné—Révolution!—pour quoi?
Une dune qui roule
Et pas une chimère où reposer ce front!
Chaque jour un désir—et deux ou trois par porte.
J'en ai couru des corps—ô fenaisons! masures!
L'aube s'écroule avec la mer.

14

Jeunes gens, pas au poète gaouri, pas à lui, ne demandez pas
     d'autographe.
Quelle calligraphie sinon déjà celle de l'adieu!
Oh ne la mêlez pas à vos chiffres qui portent des fusées, des
     terrasses, des moissons.
Car celui-là, s'il est étranger sur sa terre, comment porterait-il
     avec lui l'espérance du peuple?
Celui-là si on lui refuse sa terre comment trouverait-il une
     assise à son pas?
Et c'est là qu'on en vient aux racines,
Et c'est là que je dis : ensemble nous reboisons,
C'est là que se lève la meute
Pour aboyer non pour construire,
Pour étaler
       Non pour sécher
Le sang.
La meute qui ne sait que sourire
—Mais regardez ses dents!

Bay leaves, cumin, garlic and the drop of shade
In which the imagination simmers.
I love you—but wait, I am speaking to the void!
I gave up my love to the cicadas of Europe.
I gave up everything—Revolution!—for what?
A rolling dune
Without a mirage to rest this head on!
Every day a new desire—and two or three at every door
I chased after plenty of bodies—Oh haymaking season!
    Makeshift shanties!
Dawn and sea come crashing down together.

14

Young people, don't ask him, not him the gaouri poet, for
    autographs.
This stroke of the pen is none other than a farewell!
Oh don't confuse it with your initials that carry rockets,
    terraces, harvests.
For how could he, if a stranger in his own land, carry with
    him the people's hopes?
How could he, if denied his land, find his footing?
And that's how we come to roots,
And that's when I say: let's reforest the land together
Where now the pack of dogs rises up
To bark rather than build,
To show off,
       rather than staunch
The blood shed.
That pack that keeps on smiling and smiling
— But look at their teeth!

gaouri
>   bicot
gaouri
>   bicot
gaouri
>   bicot
youpin
>   raton
roumi
>   melon
bicot
>   gaouri
bicot
>   gaouri
bicot
>   gaouri

Si l'homme nouveau n'invente pas un vocabulaire à la
>   mesure de sa conscience
Que s'écroule l'homme nouveau.
Si la conscience de l'homme nouveau reste une salle de jeux
>   où s'affrontent les crapuleries
Que périsse l'homme nouveau.
Si le socialisme est une pommade lénifiante sous laquelle
>   demeurent les plaies
Qu'éclate le socialisme.
Si l'homme nouveau n'invente pas un langage nouveau,
S'il pourvoit le malheur de constantes misères,
Qu'il périsse, lui, son langage, sa nouveauté,
Que le feu les ravage!
De l'essence, camarades, de l'essence!
Adieu
>   Frères.
Et nous aurions pu nous aimer...

15

gaouri

     bicot[1]

gaouri

     bicot

gaouri

     bicot

yid

     raton[1]

roumi[2]

     melon[1]

bicot

     gaouri

bicot

     gaouri

bicot

     gaouri

If the new man does not forge a language worthy of his
   conscience
May the new man crumble.
If the new man's conscience remains a game room where
   crimes face-off against each other
May the new man perish.
If socialism is just a balm beneath which wounds still fester
May socialism burst apart.
If the new man does not forge a new language,
If he provides constant misery to misfortune
May he perish, him, his language, his newness,
May they be gutted by fire!
Gasoline, comrades, gasoline!
Farewell
     Brothers.
And we could have loved one another....

1 Racist terms used to refer to North African Arabs
2 Term used to refer to White Europeans

83

16

O ce chant qui depuis des siècles
Me guettait !
La misère des vieilles, la douleur
Des adolescents aux portes de Grenade
(Sur leurs lèvres la plainte de Boabdil prend feu!)
Et dans la rocaille d'Elche ce mineur qui offrit ses entrailles
    au temps.
(Le temps nous a truqué la conscience et l'oreille
—Foi mauvaise, mémoire équivoque, le
Temps nous a truqué le sang!)

17

Quand je serai mort, jeunes gens,
Vous mettrez mon corps sur la mer.
Vous écouterez la siguiriya —l'Irréparable où mon ancêtre
    arabe pleure,
Vous écouterez El Anka: «Ya dif Allah»,
Et le Concerto de Bartók—pour orchestre.
Pendant trente-sept ans j'ai tellement eu faim de beauté!
                    J'ai tellement eu faim de santé!
 Soyez patients. C'est une après-midi ensemble tandis que
Mon corps sur la mer...
Et puis dansez le twist, dansez à perdre haleine l'Afrique
    délivrée!
Le twist—et comme jadis sur le Môle: le hadaoui.
Jeunes gens, vous serez des hommes libres.
Vous construirez l'autogestion, vous construirez une culture
    sans races.
Vous comprendrez pourquoi ma mort est optimiste.
Je ne me suicide pas. Je vis

16

Oh this dirge that has stalked me
For centuries the misery of old women, the pain
Of adolescents at the gates of Grenada
(On their lips the groans of Baobdil burst into flames!)
And the miner who, on the rocky ground of Elche, offered
    his guts to time
(Time rigged our conscience and our ears
—Bad faith, questionable memory,
Time rigged our blood!)

17

When I am dead, young people,
You will place my body on the sea.
You will listen to the siguiriya— The Irreparable where my
    Arab ancestor cries,
You will listen to El Anka: "Ya dif Allah,"
And Bartók's Concerto for Orchestra.
For thirty-seven years I hungered for beauty!
I hungered for health!
Be patient. It's an afternoon spent together while
On the sea my body . . .
And then dance the twist, dance until you are breathless
    dancing the dance of freed Africa!
 Twist—as in the past on the Mole: the hadaoui.
Young people, you will be free.
You will establish self-management, you will establish a
    raceless culture.
You will understand why my death is a sign of hope.
This is not suicide. I live

Voila ma signature.

Jean Sénac

Et je mets un soleil

Alger-Pointe-Pescade, 23-26 janvier 1964

Here is my signature

Jean Sénac

And I add a sun.

Algiers and Pointe-Pescade, January 23-26 1964

PAROLES AVEC WALT WHITMAN
à Jacques Miel

1

Walt Whitman, à l'heure où autour de nous la liberté
  s'effondre comme un hôtel abandonné,
Et que de toutes parts les maquignons gagnent les hauteurs
A l'affût de notre dernière parole,
Rends-nous le souffle et cet « ardent mal de contact » dont
  nos yeux ont gardé l'orage.
Walt Whitman, les meubles sont vendus, les camarades se
  tordent de peur
Essayant de gagner à peine une brindille de jour.
Un long temps passera avant que notre cœur s'habitue aux
  rumeurs du sable
Et pourtant cette salive qui nous vient, sèche et salée, c'est
  déjà toute la mer.
Un oursin qui nous pique déchaînera comme une horloge le réveil.
Et nous crierons : soleil ! là où le bleu nous envahit.
O jours pesants en cette attente ! Nuits des pauvres répits!
O ces enfants qui jouaient à la balle avec un scarabée volant,
Cette souple oraison de muscles dans les herbes,
Ces abricots tachés non de cambouis mais de vase odorante,
Enfants noirs et dorés comme après un tournoi de seiches!
Jours de mon cœur,
Jours lointains et si proches!

Une seconde ici a des marges de siècles
Et les plongées nous donnent un vertige d'hirondelles.
O lumière! O mer! O dans tout cet espace le désir retenu!
Et les hautes murailles.
Je chante avec toi, Walt Whitman.
Le compagnon que tu attendais est venu,
Et dans ta grande barbe déjà pousse une inquiétude de
  seigle.

WORDS WITH WALT WHITMAN
to Jacques Miel

1

Walt Whitman, now as freedom collapses all around us like a
    deserted hotel,
And wheeler-dealers on all sides are reaching the heights
Eagerly awaiting our last word,
Restore our breath, and this "longing ache of contact"
    whose storms are maintained by our eyes.
Walt Whitman, the furniture has been sold off, the friends
    doubled over with fear
Trying to save the scarce sprig of daylight.
A long time must pass before our heart will become
    accustomed to the murmuring sand.
And yet that spit that comes, dry and salty, is already the sea
    itself.
An urchin that pricks us will strike like an alarm clock.
And we will cry out: Sun! Where the blue sweeps over us.
Oh oppressive days of this anticipation! Nights of little rest!
Oh these children who played ball with a flying beetle,
That supple prayer of muscles in the grass,
Those apricots stained not with grease but fragrant mud,
Dirty and golden children, like after a cuttlefish tournament!
Days of my heart,
Days both so distant and near!
Here, one second is surrounded by margins like centuries
And each dive makes us dizzy like swallows.
Oh light! Oh sea! Oh desire restrained within this whole
    space!
And these high walls.
I sing with you, Walt Whitman.
The companion you were expecting has arrived,
And within your long beard the anxious rye is already
    sprouting.

«Je n'attendais pas cette tristesse ni le consentement à la
    phrase des autres.
Je n'attendais pas cette nostalgie de lunes.
Ce que j'attendais, camarade, c'est l'athlète au salut vital
Et la parole nue, auréolée de sa liqueur.
Ce que j'attendais, lèvres à lèvres,
C'est le soleil dans un mot cru.»
Oh, Walt Whitman,
Et tu repousses mes chardons!
Il faut donc reprendre la route,
Marcher, marcher vers le cœur de l'été,
Là encore marcher et marcher vers le Centre
Et reprendre la route,
Et marcher
Et marcher.

2

Camarades lointains,
Souvenez-vous de ce que nous avons souffert,
De quelles nuits nous avons dû subir
La froide vanité,
Avant que votre nom n'éclate,
Hommes libres, hommes bons.

Notre audace ne fut que tâtonnements et colères
Et l'amère saveur de cette vérité qui nous tenait debout.
Sur nous s'abattait comme des fruits de vent
La compassion de nos amis,
Et d'innommables citadelles s'édifiaient sur notre cœur.
Nous allions vers un peu d'eau, vers un peu de lumière
—Misère, avec quelle arrogance!
(Tenir un tronçon de la route
Et devoir observer le désert alentour!)
Puis venait la solitude comme un lit jamais ouvert.

90

"I wasn't expecting this sadness nor to give consent to the
    words of others.
I wasn't expecting this moon nostalgia.
What I was expecting, camerado, was the athlete with the
    vital greeting
And the naked word, in a halo of liquor
What I was expecting, lips to lips,
Was the sun in a coarse word."
Oh Walt Whitman,
You reject my thistles!
So we must get back on the road,
Walk, walk toward the heart of the summer,
There again walk and walk towards the Center
And get back on the road,
And walk
And walk.

2

Faraway friends,
Remember what we have suffered,
What nights we have endured
The cold futility
Before your name burst forth,
Free men, good men.

Our daring was only groping and anger
And the bitter taste of this truth kept us on our feet.
The compassion of our friends
Beat down upon us like the fruit of the wind
And upon our hearts were erected the citadels that can't be named.
We were making our way toward a little water, towards a little light
--And oh, shame, with such arrogance!
(Having to hold a section of road
And observe the surrounding desert!)
Then came solitude like a bed, never before opened

Où s'abattaient les griffes des rapaces,
Sur nos bras, nous imaginions votre baiser nouveau,
Ce vin qui ne ment pas
Et dont l'ivresse est bénéfique.

Puis il fallait fermer le jour
Et par une lucarne invoquer votre venue
Afin que naissent les enfants
Et que le blé ne pourrisse pas sur l'aire.

Sans l'espérance de votre geste
Qu'aurions-nous fait, camarades si loin,
Sinon gémir et construire de larmes
Une maison inachevée?

3

Et Walt Whitman, encore une fois, derrière les remparts de
    l'Espagne,
Secouant comme une cendre ses cuisses de colombe,
Entra dans la mer jusqu'aux épaules
Et il nagea,
Et les jeunes gens le regardèrent, oubliant pour une seconde
    les Françaises en bikini.
Et je vis plus loin comme une nuée de navires,
Et droits, exténués, entre les cuivres délirants,
Trois poètes,
Federico le premier qui tenait à la main une rose et sur
    son cœur, comme un raisonnement logique, une ombre
    de balcon,
Et Miguel qui serrait encore dans son poing des feuilles de
    figuier pour son ami Ramon Sitje,
Et Blas, simple comme un tronçon de bois que la mer a
    rendu.
Trois poètes, venus de quartiers populaires, des champs,

Where the raptor's claws swooped down,
On our arms, we imagined your new kiss,
That wine whose healthy intoxication,
never lies.

Then we had to shut down the day
And through a skylight invoke your arrival
So that children could be born
And the wheat not rot on the threshing floor.

Without the hope you had pointed toward
What would we, such far-off friends, have done
Other than languish and build with tears
An unfinished house?

3

And Walt Whitman once again from behind ramparts in
    Spain,
Shaking out his dove thighs like ash,
Entered the sea to his shoulders
And swam,
And the young people watched him, forgetting for one
    second the French girls in their bikinis.
And I saw further out something like a thick cloud of ships,
Upright and exhausted among the delirious brass
    instruments,
Three poets,
First, Federico, who was holding a rose in his hand and over
    his heart, like a logical argument, a balcony's shadow,
And then Miguel who was still grasping fig leaves in his fist
    for his friend Ramon Sitje,
And finally Blas, as simple as a wooden log that the sea
    throws back.
Three poets, from working class neighborhoods, from the fields,

Chacun te célébrant, Whitman,
Tandis qu'à larges brasses ton corps harmonieux écrivait sa
    cantate
(A l'Espagne, à la liberté,
A notre nuit, hommes fragiles).

Et j'ai pris un galet,
Et longtemps je l'ai promené sur mes lèvres
Avant de dire le premier mot.

Peñiscola, août 1959

Whitman, they all extol your virtues,
While with wide breaststrokes your harmonious body wrote
   its cantata
(To Spain, to freedom,
To our night, fragile men).

And I took a stone,
And for a long, long time ran it over my lips
Before speaking the first word.

Peñiscola, August 1959

Avant-Corps

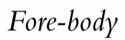

Fore-body

PREMIER POÈME ILIAQUE

1

A l'orée de ta lyre
Une cicatrice me parle
De conquêtes. Le verbe
Dans son délire nuptial
Traque le mot jusqu'à la moelle.
Sur le Môle, l'enfant s'arrache aux cotonnades
Et prélude à la nuit.

T'aimer
Serait rendre aux syllabes
Un sourire innocent.

2

Ils inventèrent la première plaie.
L'arbre y secoua ses ravines.
La nuit prit. Tout autour
La parole ne fut plus qu'un nuage tuméfié.

Amour,
Qu'allions-nous faire sur ces territoires?
Poussés par quel secret?

3

Le cerne de tes yeux et le bleu de l'épaule
          C'est toute une nuit pour mon Voyage.
Je serre dans mon point un galet. Leurs injures
Ont brisé les oursins.

THE ILIAC: THIGH POEM I

1

At the edge of your lyre
A scar speaks to me
Of conquests. Language
In its wedding fever
Tracks down the word to the bone.
On the Mole, the child frees himself from the towel;
A prelude to the night.

To love you
Would be to restore to each syllable
its innocent grin.

2

They coined the first wound.
And there the tree shook out its ravines.
The night takes hold. All around
Speech is nothing but a swollen cloud.

Love,
What were we planning to do on this plot of ground?
What secret spurred us on?

3

The dark rings of your eyes and the bruises of your shoulder
Are my whole night's Voyage.
I squeeze a tide-smoothed rock in my fist. Their curses
Have cracked the sea urchin open.

Toute la mer s'écoule
Comme si j'étais ouvert en deux.

4

Mais toi
Tu nargues le trident de cet Ordre Moral,
Tu instaures
Le tendre plaisir des rivages,
Une architecture radieuse,
Le pain et l'audace pour tous.

Vers tes hanches ce n'est pas seulement le bonheur qui augure
Ou cette grande fête des adolescents sur la digue,
Ce n'est pas seulement dans ta salive le poème comme un poisson,
Mais déjà une moisson
Armée de notre solitude.

Le jour approche où la santé
Eclatera comme un plongeon.

5

Au niveau de ton pas
Je jette mes mots fous,
Qu'ils dissolvent la boue
A tes pieds adorables
Où mes lèvres iront
Ranimer le poème,
Où mes baisers sauront
Recharner l'univers.

The sea—all of it—trickles out.
As if I were split in two.

4

But you
You scorn the trident of that Moral Code
You establish
Gentle pleasure along the coast,
A radiant architecture,
Bread and boldness for all!

It's not just happiness that I am expecting down at your hips
Or the great teenage celebration on the sea wall,
No, it's not just in your spit that the poem like a fish
Is already bounty
Armed with our loneliness.

The day is coming when good health
Will leap forward like a diver.

5

At your feet
I throw down my mad words
May they crumble the soil
At your adorable feet
Where my lips will go
To revive the poem,
Where my kisses soon
Will recarnalize the universe.

6

C'est à ce point précis où l'élan et la source
Enrichissent ma langue
  Que j'affirme, le temps d'une halte,
  Non plus mon empire lunaire
  Mais l'humble déraison d'ajuster à l'orgasme
  Le souffle même de mes mots.

7

Iliaque
Parce que là où est ta lyre
Là est mon poème,
Et mon soleil,
Immense comme une main.

Pointe-Pescade, 27 juin 1966

6

It's precisely here that the rush and the source
Enrich my tongue
     That I assert, in the time it takes to pause,
     Not my lunatic influence
     But the humble folly of matching my orgasm
     To the words I breath.

7

Thigh
Because your lyre is there
So, too, lies my poem,
And my sun,
Vast as a hand.

Pointe-Pescade, June 27th 1966

G...

Cette prise du corps non comme une bataille
Mais comme si la mer s'engouffrait dans l'entaille
Où l'âme scintillait de girelle et d'oursin.
Et ce rêve arrondi : mon poème ou ton sein?
Je ne sais plus. Le verbe au remblai des bavards
Est ce silence aigu de la chair en son dard.
Les murs eux-mêmes sont ce livre où tu m'inventes
Tandis qu'entre nos bras mille planètes ventent.
Je t'aime et je voudrais que les mots soient précis
Comme ta peau à l'heure où l'univers dit oui.

G...

To claim the body not in a blood–soaked clash
But as the sea surges up the gash
Where the soul gleams with sea urchins, wrasse,
And the rounded dream: my poem or your breast?
I know no more. Language at the wall where gossips spin
Is the razored silence of stinging skin.
The wall a book where you invented me,
While in our arms a thousand planets are set free.
I want the words *I love you* to be just as precise
As your flesh at the moment that the universe says yes.

DEUXIÈME POÈME ILIAQUE

1

Une girelle un peu d'ombre et le vœu des regards
Voilà dans l'étendue farouche du soleil
Notre halte.
D'un rocher à l'autre, d'un creux
De sable à l'angle de la digue
Les syllabes se poursuivent, les mots s'assemblent, le livre
S'épanouit.
Emerveillé, le souffle en moi frais comme un fruit de mer,
Je recopie mon vocabulaire d'été.

2

Et le mot
Comme une effusion d'eau
Prend la forme elle-même de nos corps.
Ecrire devient
Une anatomie vertigineuse
(Avec tous les risques de l'embolie
Et le plaisir patient de lever sous tes lèvres
Un sens terré).

3

J'aime écrire parce que c'est
Te couvrir de caresses,
Nommer ta chair dans son plus féroce au-delà,
Et boire, à même nos songes,
D'une même bouche épurée,
Ces mots fous de soleil et d'orange sanguine!

THE ILIAC: THIGH POEM II

1

A wrasse a little shade the wishful glance
Here in the sun's fierce expanse is
Our place to rest.
From one rock to another, from one hollow
Of sand at the edge of the sea wall
Syllables continue, words collect, the book
Blossoms.
Filled with wonder, the breath within me fresh as today's catch,
I copy down my summer vocabulary.

2

And the word
Like a current
Takes the shape of our bodies.
Writing becomes
An anatomy that leaves us spinning
(With all the risks of clots
And the patient delights of lifting from your lips
A buried meaning.)

3

I love writing because it is like
Covering you with caresses,
Naming your flesh in the fiercest world beyond,
Drinking straight from our dreams
Those wild words of sun and blood oranges
With the same mouth freed of impurities!

4

De moi à moi tu es
Le sourire qui conduit aux forges secrètes.

Armé de lunettes marines et d'un harpon bleu,
Tu captures les paroles agressives.
Au soir, nous allumons sur le sable un feu de varech
Et tu danses, juste vêtu d'un mot.

14 juillet 1966

4

From me to me you are
The smile that leads to secret forges.

Armed with water goggles and a blue harpoon,
You trap hostile words.

At night, we light a kelp fire on the sand
And you dance, dressed in a single word.

July 14th, 1966

NI LE BAISER

Dans la maison lustrale
Il y a tant de graffiti
Que les murs en sont vierges
Et de nouveau la parole possible.

Mais nous nous taisons et la mer
En nous roule, siècle après siècle,
Déchets et feux. Ce soir
Nous ne nommerons rien.

NOR THE KISS

In the lustral house
There is so much graffiti
That the walls are pure
And language possible once again.

But we stay silent and the sea
Within us rolls, century after century,
Flotsam and fire. Tonight
We will name nothing.

ÉMERSION

Ce rythme régulier de raclement de gorge
C'est la mer le poème instituant sa forge.
La nuit rien ne te vient. Mais parmi le varech
Le galet descendu de la colline avec
Les odeurs de pétrole et de piment scintille.
Tes yeux boivent. Ton corps, ému, se déshabille.
Tu plonges. Les oursins montent du petit jour.
Des mots ! Ce sont les mots dilatés de l'amour!
Tu t'accordes alors si bien à ta présence
Que les syllabes font des flammes à tes hanches.

EMERSION

The regular rhythm of clearing your throat
Is the sea, the poem stoking the forge.
At night nothing comes. But covered in kelp
The stone from the hill sparkles
Smelling of spice and oil.
Your eyes drink. Moved, your body strips.
You dive.
At daybreak the urchins rise.
Words! Swollen words of love!
Then you and your presence find such harmony
That syllables like flames lick your hips fervently.

TROISIÈME POÈME ILIAQUE

1

Tu tords ton maillot jusqu'à l'âme.
Je suis entre tes mains, ruisselant, le poème.
Et tous ces mouvements pour ajuster ton corps
Au nylon rouge, tout ce galbe
Sacralisée, immobile, éclatant,
Qu'est-ce sinon le geste du poème?
Tes jeux, tes sauts, sur les tripodes
Gravent les syllabes essentielles.

2

Seule une caméra pourrait rendre mon art poétique
Tes muscles, tes fous rires,
Ballet de signes sur les blocs.

3

Le Môle, mon cahier
D'où rituellement je ramène
Mon mythe : vos graphismes.

4

Contre leur morale révulsée
La gloire pudique de vos corps.

114

THE ILIAC: THIGH POEM III

1

You wring the soul out of your swimsuit.
I am the poem, dripping wet, in your hands
And all the movement needed to fit red nylon
to your body, this shapely leg
Made sacred, immobile, dazzling.
What is it if not the gestures of a poem?
Your games, leaping from island to island
Inscribe essential syllables.

2

Only a movie camera could make my art poetic:
Your muscles, your fits of laughter,
Dance of signs on blocks of paper.

3

The Mole, my notebook
From which I ritually bring back
My myth: your penmanship.

4

Against their offended morality
The chaste glory of your bodies.

5

A chaque pore une note.
Au bout du voyage le chant.

21 juillet 1966

16

5

For each pore a note.
At the end of the voyage the song.

July 21st, 1966

INTERROGATION

1

Je croyais qu'on mangeait les mots
(dit Antar), qu'on les mastiquait lèvres à lèvres
—gomme non pour effacer mais pour que ta salive
déchaîne ses reflux en moi, gomme pour...
Je savais (dit Lila) que les mots n'étaient pas des fruits,
que les poètes mentaient (une casserole sur le balcon soudain
se décrochait, s'affalait sur le sable—rires, ou brouhaha—
Lila se mordait le poignet).
Pas des fruits (dit Antar)
mais comme un besoin, une urine.
Pour rien alors (dit Bilâl).
Un besoin (Antar). Donc ni utiles ni nécessaires (Bilâl,
obsédé des possibilités de la derbouka—son aguet de butor
    —sa surprise vers les roseaux).
Un besoin c'est capital (dit Lila en ramenant de l'eau de
    mer).

2

(Intervenait toujours pour forcer les visages—leur donner
    force—à vaincre leurs routines d'ombre, pour
    muscler les syllabes, des hanches vers...) Les mots
    sont des cuisses (dit Yahia—puis se tut. Bilâl pesait
    de son sourire sur la nuit. Sortit—braguette à la
    merci de toutes les étoiles). Les mots sont des cuisses
    (Bilâl sentait en lui...) Les mots ...

INTERROGATION[1]

1

I thought that words were eaten
(says Antar), that they were chewed and passed from lip to lip
—gum not for erasing but so your spit can be let loose in
    me, gum for...
I knew (says Lila) words weren't fruit, that poets lied
    (suddenly a pot on the balcony came off its hook, and
    fell down on to the sand—laughter, or confusion—
Lila was biting her cuff).
Not fruit (says Antar)
but like a basic need, like urine.
For nothing then (says Bilâl).
A need (Antar). Therefore neither useful nor necessary
    (Bilâl, obsessed with the possibilities of the doumbek—
    his heron's look-out post—
surprised in the reeds).
A need is essential (says Lila as she brings water back from the sea).

2

(Always intervening to force expression—to give them strength—
to conquer their shadowy routines, to build the muscles of

---

1 This poem is from a section titled "Diwân du Noûn" : Corpoème ["Diwân of
Noûn": Corpoem]. The epigraph for this section of *Fore-body* reads:

"At Pointe-Pescade (Algiers) by the sea, some young people and the Master of
Noûn spent their nights conversing, building the dream, living their summer
intensely. Whereas all around them (the beach, the room) and within them the
Battle with the Angel (with Man) raged on.

Noûn is the Arabic letter N that mysteriously begins a sura of the Koran and
whose mythic form, ن , opens onto the sign of the Two Earths.

The character ؏ ...is an irony point."

3

Cuisses. Si donc Jacob s'arc-boute et prend assise
Sur le cri des pleureuses ou la surprise
D'un berger entre deux roseaux,
L'Ange tamponne sa peau
D'une consonne bleue où le combat s'éclaire :
Pour qui sait lire il y a là toute l'injustice du Père,
Ses tricheries, la corde, la glu dans le pommier ;
L'Ange ne fait que rappeler
La première impudence et sur la hanche exalte
Ce chant de dérision en un chiffre de basalte.
Nous l'appellerons Noûn.

4

Une impropriété car l'ongle
Qui entre dans la chair est un soc. Le sillon
Qu'elle creuse (dit Antar) est prolifération de pus, une
    absence de carnation.
Ooooh (dit Bilâl) si on allait se taper un bain?
Et nous parlerons de nos ongles (dit Lila),
Parlerons? (dit Bilâl) Nous jouerons avec!

5

C'est un sein, une route en marche, une circonférence en
    action...
Le grand circoncis ٩(dit Bilâl)

syllables, of iliac verses...) Words are thighs (says Yahia—and
then was quiet. Bilâl was pressing his smile against the night.
Went out—with his fly at the mercy of the stars.) Words are
thighs (Bilâl felt within himself...) Words...

3

Thighs. Therefore if Jacob presses against and latches onto
The cry of the hired mourners or the surprise
Of a shepherd between two reeds,
The Angel dabs his skin
With a blue consonant in which the struggle is made clear:
The Father's injustice is there for anyone to see
His cheating tricks, the rope, the bird line in the apple tree;
The Angel is only a reminder of
The original act of impudence and the hip extols
With initials carved in basalt this mocking song.
Let's call it Noûn.

4

A mistake because the fingernail
That digs into flesh is a ploughshare. The furrow
That it digs (says Antar) is festering with pus, and drains the
    skin of color.
Oooh (says Bilâl) how about we go for a swim?
And we'll talk about our nails (says Lila).
Talk? (says Bilâl) We'll play with them!

5

It's a breast, a road on the march, a circumference in action...
The great circumcised man ۶ (says Bilâl)
...It is (continued Yahia) the will of Sagittarius, the star and

...C'est (reprit Yahia) la volonté du Sagittaire, l'étoile et la
   flèche, le cancer ...
L'étoile et le croissant (dit Lila), toute l'audace de la nuit
   recueillie en un signe.
La terre et le soleil, la lune, l'orbite (dit Antar) du premier
   mot, du dernier mot, autour de l'œil.
Le Noûn! (Qui donc au juste dit ?)
Une trace de Dieu sur l'ongle, Mais Dieu, mais l'ongle? (dit
   Yahia).

6

Sur son rocher le génie du Noûn
Armait son harpon, toussait.
Personne n'y prenait garde. Alors
Il retirait son slip, dans l'effusion des cris
Plongeait.

On voyait son petit corps nu, ce fuseau d'oranges fuser
Vers un colloque de girelles.

Parfois son rire à la surface crevait la transparence.
(Puis repartait—Son plongeon comme une sourate sur le
   bandeau d'une mosquée.)

7

Car tu es troupeau et nous t'avons marqué au Noûn.
Mais se rebiffe Jacob et la ruse de l'Homme
Ne touche pas sa chair au-delà des caniveaux
Où les siècles croupissent—les terribles oiseaux
Echappent à Dieu, leur vol le tance—,
Où les siècles blanchissent hors de la transparence,
Filent une trame policière, un écran, un labyrinthe
Où Jacob feint parfois de projeter ses plaintes
Mais Tout se passe ailleurs vers cet autre alphabet
Dont Dieu n'a jamais pu approcher le secret.

122

the arrow, cancer....
The star and the crescent (says Lila), all the night's daring
    combined into one sign
The earth and the sun, the moon, the orbit around the eye
    of the first word and last (says Antar).
Noûn! (Who was it that said?)
A trace of God on a nail.   But God, but the nail? (says
    Yahia).

6

On the rocks armed with a spear,
The spirit of Noûn was coughing.
No one was paying attention. So
He took off his trunks and in the outpouring of cries
Dived in.

You could see his naked little body, that spindle of oranges, spinning
Toward a school of wrasse.

Sometimes his laugh pierced the transparent surface.
(Then went off again—His dive like a sura on a Mosque's frieze.)

7

For you are the flock and with Noûn we have branded you.
But Jacob rebels and Man's cunning
Does not touch his flesh beyond the gutters
Where centuries stagnate—the terrible birds
Escape God, their flight taunts him—
Where the centuries turn innocent. From the transparency,
are spun a detective yarn, a screen, a labyrinth
Where Jacob sometimes pretends to cast his complaints
But Everything happens elsewhere towards that other alphabet
Whose secret God has never been able to approach.

8

Et c'est là que Jacob est vainqueur. La cohorte
Des Anges peut lacérer ses côtes ; comme sur une porte
L'Homme (l'Ange privilégié, le chef)
Tambouriner de la nuit à l'aube, plaquer des tampons, bref,
Hurler tout un alphabet d'Eden et sa cabale
Dans le sang même de Jacob prostré, que dalle!
Dieu—à cette réponse qu'il implore—n'a pas accès
Et se consume dans sa création comme en un abcès.

9

(Bilâl écoute, cessant de remonter son pantalon à taille basse.
C'est comme si la mer ou quelque Ange frôlait
Sa tignasse.
Prodige que la pensée—une si vaste divagation!—
S'écrive, comme au revers de son crâne, en mots communs, courus,
Avec ces mots inanimés tellement ils ont servi
—Mais crus et tout de même utilisables.)

10

Et moi (dit Antar) une fois mangés, les mots,
Je n'sais pas si on les digère.
N'est-ce pas eux qui nous font ces cloques sur la peau
Au matin lorsqu'on se réveille?

11

Ou les moustiques ⸲(dit Lila).

12

Il prenait certains chewing-gums pour des papillons de nuit, il...
Vers la Réserve une lanterne demeurait toute la nuit—sur

124

And this is where Jacob triumphs. The hordes
Of Angels can slash his ribs; Drumming from night to dawn on
Man (the favored Angel, the chief)
like a door, pounding inkpads, in brief,
Screaming out a whole Edenic alphabet and its cabal
In a prostrate Jacob's very blood, nothing!
God—to that implored for answer—has no access
And is consumed within his creation as if in an abscess.

9

(Bilâl listens, no longer pulling up his low-riding pants.
It is as if the sea or some Angel was ruffling
His mop of hair.
A miracle, that thought—such vast ramblings!—
Is written, as if on the back of his skull, in plain, popular words,
Words almost lifeless from overuse
—Yet believed and despite it all still useful.)

10

And me (says Antar) I don't know
If the words once eaten can be digested.
Isn't that what causes those blisters
When we get up in the morning?

11

Or it's mosquitos ؟(says Lila).

12

He mistook wads of chewing gum for moths, he...
Towards the Reserve a lantern remained all night—on that

cette terrasse où des ivrognes inventaient un vocabulaire
... de Pointe ؏

... il... claquait des mains: ces moustiques!

Les chewing-gums qu'il collait sur des murs tout autour de
son lit, moules du souffle, de l'haleine, argile des paroles
non prononcées, pensées, pierres écrites d'un vécu qui ne
sera jamais transmis, fruits clos, forclos, des marquées au
sceau d'Onan,

il

allait comme ses papillons de nuit

vers le Noûn

et s'y brûlait la langue.

13

Tu veux un autographe

L'enfant du Noûn entrebâilla la serviette de couleurs qui lui
ceignait les reins,

et brandissant son sexe:

Tu veux un autographe

14

Les blocs du Môle ne se sont pas fendus cet après-midi—là,
ni les tripodes, ni l'immense cheminée de la cimenterie
en face.

Et il fallut que l'enfant toujours nu, impudique, fût pris du
désir baroque d'une serviette —rideau d'un théâtre d'où
allait cingler vers nos os la seule réplique qui annonçait
l'été,

la preuve (dit Yahia).

15

La preuve de quoi? (dit Bilâl).

De l'écriture, je suppose, de quelque mystère enfoui sous des
syllabes, quels alcools (dit Antar).

126

terrace where the drunks came up with a vocabulary
...of the Pointe ؟
...he...was clapping his hands: those mosquitoes
The chewing gum that he stuck to the walls all around his
    bed, molded breath, inspiration, the clay of unsaid
    words, thoughts, stones written by a life experience
    that will never be passed on, closed fruit, foreclosed,
    odes stamped with the seal of Onan,
he
went like his moths
towards Noûn
and burned his tongue on it.

                            13

You want an autograph
The child of Noûn left the multi-colored towel that girded
    his loins half opened and his genitals brandished:
You want an autograph

                            14

That afternoon the blocks of the Mole were not cracked nor
    were the islands off the coast or the immense chimney of
    the cement works across the way.
And the still naked and immodest child had to be seized by
    the strange desire for a
towel—it is the curtain in a theater where the only line
    announcing summer's arrival would come full tilt
    towards our bones,
the proof (says Yahia).
                            15

The proof of what? (says Bilâl).
Of the written word, I suppose, of some mystery buried

                                                    127

Du poème et du corps, du corps écrit, du Corpoème (dit
    Yahia).

16

Et Jacob déjà grattait à l'ongle la marque
Du Ciel, envenimée de mouches bavardes, de parques,
Grattait au canif l'arc-en-ciel purulent
Dont les poètes allaient l'habiller, ce chiendent
Dont Delacroix a fait un cèdre, cet érésipèle :
L'Ange et Jacob—si beau avec au flanc l'ombre épanouie
    d'une aile!

17

Tout ça (dit Lila) ça se passait du côté de la Palestine arabe?
    Mais cette nuit-là (dit Bilâl) Dieu appela Jacob : Israël!

18

Et tous nous avons vaincu Dieu! Jacques sur son tracteur,
    Patrick dans sa Ballade—et Mohamed à Médine, non?

    Cette Palestine c'est ici, c'est notre île aux chardons,
    c'est Nanterre, le Viêt-Nam, Peñiscola, la «Cafet» ou
    Damas. Tiens, Yahia, c'est sur ton îlot (dit Antar). Quand
    on y entraîne des filles, ces lits de plumes (d'éponges)
    dans le roc, ça n'est pas la trace du combat?
Cet Israël, regarde, c'est ce lit, cette taie qui fuit. Prends cette
    plume: c'est pas la preuve que cette nuit même un Ange?...

beneath the syllables, what alcohol (says Antar).
Of the poem and the body, of the written body, of the
  Corpoem (says Yahia).

16

And Jacob was already scratching at
Heaven's mark with his nail, infected with the chattering
  flies, with the Fates,
He scratched with a penknife the suppurating rainbow
With which poets would dress him, that twitch grass
Which Delacroix turns into a cedar tree, that Saint
  Anthony's fire:
The Angel and Jacob—so beautiful with the blooming hint
  of a wing on his side!

17

All this (says Lila) was going on near Arab Palestine?
But that night (says Bilâl), God called Jacob: Israël!

18

And all of us have conquered God! Jacques on his tractor,
  Patrick in his Ballad—and Mohamed at Medina, right?

  That Palestine is here, it is our island of thistles, it is
  Nanterre, Vietnam, Peñiscola, "la Cafet", or Damascus.
  Hey, Yahia, it is on your small island (says Antar.) When
  we bring girls there those beds of feathers (of sponges) in
  the rocks, aren't they traces of the battle?
That Israel, look, it's this bed, this pillowcase that is fleeing.
  Take this feather: isn't that proof that on this very night
  an Angel?...

19

Ce Gué de Jabbok, cette Médina, c'est ce livre. Et je l'ai dans
    ma main (dit Lila), il parle sur mon cœur, comme un galet
    de quatre sous!

20

Il y met une telle frénésie ce boiteux
Qu'il va bien boiter à la fin avec le cri de Dieu
Ouvert à son flanc comme un livre!
Il n'y a rien à lire, mais lui, ivre
De toute cette nuit engloutie en lui, brode
Toute une histoire, et un vocabulaire avec des mots larges
    comme des tripodes.
Où les baigneurs viennent coincer leur pied.
Il boite, alors il faut que tous on boite, et sa plaie
Il en fait un piège où notre plaisir sombre.
Allez vite vous rhabiller et passez du soleil à l'ombre!
S'il croit que nous allons nous laisser prendre à son chloroforme,
Que notre bouche de sa plaie va prendre la forme
Pour répéter que Dieu est fort et que nous l'avons vaincu
Mais qu'à la fin des fins c'est nous qui l'avons dans l'écu,
Eh bien le grand Monsieur Jacob il se trompe,
Et si nous devons emboucher une trompe
C'est pour célébrer la joie d'un reflet dans l'eau
Et le simple bonheur d'une peau qui se colle à une autre peau!

21

Si vous saviez, la peau d'un Ange, dit Jacob ٩ (dit Bilâl).

19

This Jabbok's Ford, this Medina, is this book. And I have it
    in my hand (says Lila), I feel it within me, like a four-
    cent stone!

20

This lame man goes about things so frenetically
That in the end he will still be limping with God's cry
Opened on his side like a book!
There is nothing to read there, but drunk
On this entire night engulfed within him, he weaves
An entire story, and vocabulary with words as big as the
    islands off the coast.
Where swimmers get their feet caught.
He limps, so all of us have to limp and his wound
He turns it into a trap in which our pleasure founders.
Quickly put your clothes back on and move into the shade!
If he thinks we are going to get caught with his chloroform,
That our mouths are going to take the shape of his wound
To repeat that God is strong and that we have conquered
    him
And in the end emblazoned him on our shields
Well, the great Mr. Jacob has bungled
And if we have to put our mouths to our bugles
It is to celebrate the joy of reflections in the water
And the simple pleasures of skin pressed against skin!

21

If you only knew, an Angel's skin, says Jacob ؏ (says Bilâl)

L'enfant du Noûn, très loin de ce combat,
Plongeait de la digue des Turcs.

Lunettes, palmes, il fouillait l'eau
De son sourire
Et parfois ramenait
Une dorade.

(Des chenilles passaient sur la route, traînant des canons. Vers
    Jabbok.)
Gaza, ô ma gazelle, est prise! (avait chante Lila. Et vers
    Peniel nous engagions nos armes.)

Il suffisait d'ouvrir le balcon,
De descendre sur la plage,
De se dénuder comme un empereur pour le sacre,
Et d'avancer.
Là il y a Bougie, là Tigzirt,
Là Hyères,
Ici Ilion,
Là Beyrouth, là Alexandrie,
Là Peñiscola,
Ici Gênes (Jacques tu t'en souviens—et ce banc sous les
    palmes, le rôdeur nocturne, les poires volées?),
Ici Gibraltar, là, mon cœur, Ithaque
La route est vaste, libre. La nuit claire.

Il suffirait d'avoir la force.

22

The child of Noûn, far from this battle,
Dove from the Turk's sea wall.

Mask, flippers, he searched the water
With his smile
And at times brought back
A sea bream.

23

(Caterpillars moved along the road, dragging cannons.
    Towards Jabbok.)
Gaza, oh my gazelle, has been captured! (Lila had sung. And
    towards Peniel we commit our arms.)

24

All you had to do was to open the doors to the balcony,
Go down to the beach,
Disrobe like an emperor at his coronation,
And move forward.
There is Bougie, there is Tigzirt
There is Hyères,
There is Ilion,
There Beirut, there Alexandria.
There is Peñiscola,
Here Genoa, (Jacques, do you remember—and that bench
    under the palm trees, the nocturnal prowler, the stolen pears?),
Here Gibraltar, there my dear, Ithaca,
The road is wide and free. The night is clear.

All you need is the strength.

Voilà (dit Yahia). C'est pourquoi moi aussi j'aime la mer.
L'espace est offert. Il n'y a pas d'obstacle.

Il y a la mer (dit Lila).

C'est vrai, il suffirait (Bilâl épatait son nez à la vitre).

25

Et la plaie en une rose d'écume s'épanouit et brille.
Syllabes effervescentes, ô mangeur de lentilles!
Faut-il que nous soyons tous fascinés
Par quelle atroce nostalgie pour croire à ton ciné,
Et comme Tiski ou Timour sentir que notre tendon se brise
A l'instant de l'élan, que quelqu'un à sa guise
Taillade et creuse comme sur une ardoise le mot
Non pas de passe mais d'impasse! Sommes-nous sots
Pour consentir soudain à écrire de notre inquiétude cette fable,
Ce sablier tourné et retourné, ce sable
A perte de mémoire qui nous glisse comme une moelle entre
    les syllabes,
Ce sang!

26

Plutôt que de perdre la raison, les poètes appellent à la rescousse
(dit Yahia) leurs pairs et fouillent dans leurs mots. Fouinent. Une
image, c'est sur leur front un chiffon de vinaigre. Une diversion.
La folie patiente. On peut repartir pour des émotions. Jusqu'à
l'heure où finalement on perd pied dans l'espace. Il ne reste plus
qu'à hurler: —le seul mot sauvé du désastre!—«Crénom!»

26 *bis*

(Pour tel autre, l'éternité commença à l'orgasme. Belle mort !
    On voit (dit Lila) que tu n'étais pas à la place de la fille !)

There (says Yahia). This is why I also love the sea.
It gives you space. It presents no obstacles.
There is the sea (says Lila).
It is true, it's all you need (Bilâl pressed his nose to the glass).

25

And the wound blooms into a rose of foam and shines.
Effervescent syllables, oh lentil eaters!
Must we all be fascinated
By some horrible nostalgia in order to be taken in by your theatrics
And like Tiski or Timour feeling that our tendons are tearing
As we gain momentum , that someone as if on a blackboard
Slashes and digs not the password
But the impasse! Are we fools
For suddenly consenting to write this fable out of our anxiety,
This hour glass is turned over and over, this sand
To oblivion that slides like marrow between syllables!
This blood!

26

Rather than losing their minds, poets call for help (says Yahia) from
their peers and dig through their words. They nose about. An
image, is on their foreheads like a vinegar compress. A diversion.
Patient madness. We can start out again for emotions. Until the
moment when finally we lose our footing in space. All that remains
is to scream—the only phrase salvaged from the disaster!—"What
in God's name!"

26 *bis*

(For others, eternity began with the orgasm. Beautiful
    death! We see (says Lila) that you weren't in the girl's
    place!)

Et ce Baudelaire, n'est-il pas, lui, le Maître de tes Mots ? Tu nous cites toujours Char (ton Dieu), Artaud, Genet, Otero, Hikmet, Voznessenski, Ginsberg, Retamar, Whitman, Lorca, Verlaine, Eluard, Rimbaud, Louise Labé, Aragon, Brecht— mais ce Baudelaire dont tu ne nous parles jamais et, qu'avec Racine, tu relis chaque soir ? (dit Lila).

«Et plus tard un Ange, entrouvrant les portes...», n'est ce pas avec ces mots que ton corps a grandi? (reprit Yahia. Et nouant sa serviette de bain autour de son front, il s'en fit le Turban des Doges).

28

(«... cette séduisante vigueur des corps souples...» En se déployant sur la natte, Bilâl entrait tout cru dans la phrase de Proust.)

29

(Le Maitre du Noûn, las de la mer, s'approcha d'eux, les caressait.)

30

Enfants, enfants, enfants (dit-il comme s'il les enfantait).

31

Alors la plaie comme un arc se tendit
Et la cohorte des mots...

32

Louange.

27

And that Baudelaire, isn't he the Master of your Words? You are always quoting Char (your God), Artaud, Genet, Otero, Hikmet, Voznesenki, Ginsberg, Retamar, Whitman, Lorca, Verlaine, Eluard, Rimbaud, Louis Labé, Aragon, Brecht—but that Baudelaire whose name you never mention and you reread every night along with Racine? (says Lila).

"And later an Angel, cracking open the doors..." isn't it with these words that your body grew? (continued Yahia. And tying his beach towel around his head, made a Doge's Turban).

28

("...that seductive vigor of supple bodies..." In spreading himself out on his mat, Bilâl directly entered into Proust's phrase.)

29

The Master of Noûn, tired of the sea, approached them, was caressing them.

30

Children, children, children (he said as if he were giving birth to them).

31

And then the wound bent like a bow
And droves of words...

32

Praise.

TRIOMPHE OU DÉRISION DU MOT
(onzain)

Tu as reçu ton nom. Tu es purifié.
Et
Moi
J'erre,
Nomade sans Jabbok,
Persécuteur sans Damas,
Prophète sans Médine,
Epave.
Il suffirait pourtant que de ma bave,
Au détour d'un tripode, l'Homme se lève et que je sois
Nommé !

Pointe-Pescade, 22 mai-24 juin 1967

TRIUMPH OR MOCKERY OF THE WORK
(Eleven-lined stanza)

You have received your name. You are purified.
And
Me
I wander,
A Nomad with no Jabbok,
Persecutor with no Damascus,
Prophet with no Medina,
Wreckage.
And yet all it takes is for a Man to rise up from my foaming mouth
By way of the islands off shore, for me to be
Named!

Pointe-Pescade, May 22-June 24 1967

Le Myth du Sperme-
Méditerranée

The Myth of the Mediterranean-Semen

LA STÈLE

Je ne réagis plus, d'accord;
D'une voix a peine murmurante,
Sur les vingt-six plaies de mon corps
Je dresse la stèle de malédiction.

Venez lire, camarades!
Lâches et châtrés de tous bords,
Mâles fumellisés et fumelles malignes,
Sur l'obélisque de mes torts!

Qu'elle est chaude cette odeur de mort,
—Mes nuages!—l'orgasme qui nie
(Vos meubles!) Que grouillent vos progénitures (ornements
    de la Bombe, panache)!

Les sexes voyous sur ma peau
Mettent leurs désordres en fresque.
Venez voir, camarades, il n'y a pas dans vos putains de vies
    d'aussi belle légende!

THE STELE

I don't react anymore, fine;
Instead in barely a whisper
I plant the stele of malediction
Atop my body's twenty-six wounds.

Come read, comrades!
The cowards and castrati.
Effeminized males and malleable females.
Read the obelisk of my errors!

How hot is the stench of death,
—My clouds!—the orgasm that denies
(Your tangible assets!) How your progeny swarm
(Ornaments on an A-bomb shot with flair)!

The cocks of street trash
Show-off their disorder in epic fashion
Come see, comrades, in your whole god damn lives
Have you ever seen a more beautiful legend!

LA CORDE

Dieu dans mes couilles met à l'affût
Adam, Jacob et Job—et l'ange juif
Et l'ange arabe. Il m'a nommé
Provocateur du foutre pour que les étoiles
Tombent une à une sur l'Assemblée
—La brûlent—sur les villas—les brûlent!—les HLM.
Si les Chinois ne viennent pas, je viendrai
Rétablir le Pain.

Les abricots remontent à la surface
—Rires éclats!—riches de dorades.
A s'y frotter la peau devient un lait.

—Le cœur un oursin!
Ginsberg, viens, attachons nos barbes.
Fabriquons une corde de conscience-choc contre leurs
ventouses.

Ils ont forts. Abjectement. Et beaux!

II n'y a pas d'âme. Mais il y a des torrents de pus sous la peau

Du soleil !

THE ROPE

God in my balls has
Adam, Jacob and Job lying in wait—and the Jewish angel
And the Arab angel. He named me
Provocateur of Come so that the stars might
Fall one by one onto the Assembly
—Burn it—on the villas—burn them!—the housing projects.
If the Chinese don't arrive, I'll show up
To restore the Bread.

Apricots float to the surface
—Bursts of laughter!—teeming with sea bream.
By rubbing against it, skin turns to milk.

—The heart, a sea urchin!
Ginsberg, come, let's tie our beards together.
Let's braid a rope of conscious-shock to keep out those
    blood-suckers.

They're strong. Despicably. And beautiful!

There is no soul. Only streams of pus beneath the skin

Sunlight!

LA COURSE

Tu parles d'amour et d'amour. Je ne comprends
Que la douleur des couilles qui n'ont que leur miroir
Pour se vider. Tu parles de cheveux blonds, de poitrines
Civilisées. Je ne comprends

Que le sexe qui vrombit à vide sur les rocs.
Il y a des motos énormes adolescentes qui dérapent
Sur l'os iliaque. Et des continents qui
Affleurent sous les tripots du cri.

Je ne comprends
Que les larmes où bafouillent des soucoupes volantes.
Et des noms: Ahmed! Mahrez! Kamel! Antar!
Oh, encule-moi! O Youcef, j'ai sucé jusqu'au Coran
Ta course. Maintenant sur le sable

Tu rentres dans le sablier. Tu coules
A pic. Quel océan a pris ta place?
Quelle planète habille ta queue?
Le feu est invisible. Tu sais qu'il bouge aux cendres du
        poème. Je ne comprends
Que la douleur du sexe-boomerang.
Tu nous parles d'amour, d'amour, d'amour comme une
        momie qui déroule ses litanies d'or,
Sa pustule. Je ne comprends
Que l'abyssale douleur des couilles
Qui refusent la déperdition.
Plutôt le Vide que le Trou,
Le Vide où peut croiser la Masse-Compacte-Spirituelle,
Seul Présent concevable. Papa passé tu parles. Je ne
        comprends
Que le ciel et la mer accouplés, jumeaux

146

THE RACE

You speak of love and of love again. I don't understand
Anything but the pain of balls mirrored
So they can be drained. You speak of blond hair, the chests of
Civilized people. I don't understand

Anything but pricks that run on empty.
Enormous adolescent motorcycles that skid
Across thighs. And continents
Rising from under this lair of screams.

I don't understand
Anything but the tears where flying saucers stammer.
And names: Ahmed! Mahrez! Kamel! Antar!
Oh, fuck me! Oh Youcef, I have sucked your race
As far as the Koran. Now on the sand

You enter the hour glass. On cue
You begin to flow. What ocean took your place?
What planet trusses your cock?
The fire is invisible. It moves, you know, according to the
    poem's ashes. I don't understand
Anything but the agony of boomerang-cocks.
You speak to us of love, of love, of love like a mummy
    unwinding its golden litanies,
Its pustule. I don't understand
Anything but the bottomless pain of balls
That reject loss.
The Void but not the Hole,
Where the Compact-Spirit-Mass can cross,
The only conceivable Present. Father of long ago you are
    speaking.
I don't understand anything, but the sky and sea mating, blue

Bleus, licorne.

Oooooo exil!
L'abyssale douleur jusqu'à l'Os.

Twins, unicorn.

Oooooo exile!
Bottomless pain shot straight to the Bone.

LES GARGOTES SOMMEILLENT

Les gargotes sommeillent. Gargouillis et slogans
Veillent
(Sous pyramidales gargouilles).

Oulla ! Rien n'est plus lourd
Que ton sexe froid sur mon front.

Nous devons révéler au monde
Que le Diwân s'est mis en route
Et que bientôt les murs seront détruits.

THE GREASY-SPOONS SLUMBER

The greasy spoons slumber,
While under their gargoyles shaped like pyramids,
The night's rumblings and slogans keep watch.

Oulla! Nothing weighs more on me
Than your cold cock against my face.

Together, we must show the world
The Diwân has set out
And that soon, soon, the walls will come crashing down.

DES VIERGES VONT SE DONNER

Des Vierges vont se donner pour la Grande Orgie des
    Roseaux.

Les lèvres (lavées de la mort) gorgées de mots
Elles donneront naissance aux fils multiples de la race sans Père.

Je vous dis que le soleil va verdir
Et par transparence sur tous les ventres purs chanter
AégoO! AégoO!

VIRGINS WILL OFFER THEMSELVES

Virgins will offer themselves to the Great Orgy of the
  Reeds.

With their lips gorged with words, scrubbed free of death,
They will bear son after son of a Fatherless race.

I'm telling you that, the blood will drain from the sun's face
Leaving no trace on their unsullied bellies and it will sing:
AégoO! AégoO!

AAAAAAA…

Tout est foutu—les comités de gestion, le rire, nos
    érections?
Tout?
(Le Chenoua s'est cassé; sur les boulevards les bien-rasés
    portent ses morceaux en pochette.)
Il nous reste la mort pour mettre debout une vie.

Même secouée de breloques
Qu'elle était belle la Révolution en chaleur!
Elle a perdu son homme. Elle hurle
Entre deux somnifères—et moi aussi.
Aaaaaaaaaaaaaaaaaaaaaaaaah!
Sexes. Sexes. J'ai trouve des sexes, des sexes.
Où est l'homme?
La femme a-t-elle péri lors des dernières invasions?

AAAAAAA...

Everything's fucked—management committees, laughter,
    our erections?
Everything?
(Chenoua has been torn apart; the well-shaved men along
    the boulevards wear its pieces in their breast pockets.)
We're left with death so we can get a life.

The Revolution in heat! How beautiful she was!
Even when shaking with amulets.
She lost her man. Between two sleeping pills
She screams—and so do I,
Aaaaaaaaaaaaaaaaaaah!
Cocks! Cocks! I found cocks and more cocks
But where is the man?
And the woman, did she die at the time of the last invasion?

JAAAAAAAAAA....

Jaaaaaaaaaaaaaaaaaaaaaaaaaaaaaaaaaaaaaaaaaaaaaaaaaaaaacques!
Les pins et les sapins, les orties sous la mer
Tordent leurs fruits. Jaaaaaaaacques!

Le rêve-au-bois-dormant ronfle. Notre guitare
A refoutu le camp vers sa forêt. Ta Volkswagen
N'est pas amphibie. Je n'ai aimé
Que pour échouer sur l'espace bleu
BLEU de la solitude
—O négation liquide, Mère!

Avec les décombres de mes barques
J'ai construit le vaisseau amiral.
Jaaaaaaaaaaaaaaacques, il coule!

BSM, Pointe-Pescade, 23 août 1967

JAAAAAAAAAA....

Jaaaaaaaaaaaaaaaaaaaaaaaaaaaaaaaaaaaaaaaaaaaaaaaaaaacques!
Pines and lupines, nettles under the sea
Twisting their fruit. Jaaaaaaaacques!

My dreaming sleeping-beauty snores.
And once again our guitar
Has gotten the hell out of here
and fled to the forest. Your Volkswagen
Is not amphibious. I have loved only
So that I might be marooned in blue space
BLUE of loneliness
—Oh liquid negation, Mother!

From the wreckage of my craft
I raised a flagship.
Jaaaaaaaaaaaaaaaacques, it's going down.

BSM, Pointe-Pescade, August 23, 1967

157

LE RADEAU DE LA MÉDUSE

Le radeau de la Méduse, Vénus et Mars qui jappent
Pour aboutir au Louvre ?
L'amour en papouillis, l'amour en papoua,
En parigoterie, greenwicherie, chiennerie de palabres,
    chieries,
Esclavage, reddition—l'homme est rendu, sexe et grimoires,
    la Fumelle le tapisse, pisse dans sa bouche, se couche
Dans ses dents. Tandis que très très loin, entre l'aube et
    l'horizon, pleure
La femme.

(Très douce sans venin, complément-mon-égale, l'homme-
vaginivore, l'homme-vaginisé, t'a jetée aux Vagins. Femme
pillée et répudiée ! Autour de nous la Fumelle frappe et
fume.)

THE RAFT OF THE MEDUSA

The Raft of the Medusa, Venus and Aries are bitching
To manouevre a place in the Louvre ؟
Love with titillation, love in Tahitian
In Parisian, in Greenwich Villagese, in the endless empty
    wheeze of diarrhease
Slavery, surrender—the man is rendered, cock and balls,
    magical spells, the she-male hovers to cover him
and pisses down his mouth, then kisses
Further south. While far, far away, between the break of day and
the horizon, the lady
Wails.

(Venomless, tender, my–equal–completion,
 Depiliated and repudiated lady thrown to the Cunts
 By the cuntivore-, cuntrified-man! Around us the She-
    male smote and smoked.)

LES BEAUX BORDELS

Les gosses n'ont pas été créés pour jeter des pierres aux
    barbus
Ni pour insulter les poètes.
Mais vous avez entassé dans leur cerveau vos pourritures,
Vous en avez fait cette petite racaille hurlante sur mon
    ombre.
(Ni les chats ni les chiens pour vos Cayenne-appartements,
Et vous en avez fait des bibelots fétides.)

Dieu, si tu es, monte, qu'est-ce que tu fous?
Tout l'homme est sens dessus dessous,
Caméléonisé sur son arbre à châtrures.
Regarde comme il s'installe dans sa ruine et sa pestilence
    (avec ses p'tits moteurs, ses p'tites machines, ses p'tits zin-
    zins, ses p'tites za-zas).
Regarde comme il grignote la cervelle du voisin,
Avec quelle méthode dans nos chambres il plaque ses
Auschwitz, ses Dresde, ses Hiroshima, ses villa Susini.

Regardez, bande de cons!
Mais il n'y a plus d'Œil, plus d'yeux,
Que des anus repus par où s'engouffre la belle morale!

FANTASTIC FUCK-UPS

Kids weren't born to throw stones at men with long beards
Or insult poets.
But you have stuffed their heads with putrid thoughts,
You have transformed them into stinking knick-knacks.
You have turned them into petty scum, snarling at my
    shadow.
(Not the cats or dogs of your prison apartments).

God, if you exist, get up here, what the hell are you doing?
Man is strung upside down,
Chameleonized on his tree of castration.
See how he settles into his stench and ruin
(with his l'il motors, his l'il machines, his l'il thingamajigs,
    his l'il thingamabobs).

See how he nibbles at his neighbor's brain,
How he methodically dumps in our room his
Auschwitzes, his Dresdens, his Hiroshimas, his Villa Susini

Look you goddamn idiots!
There's no keyholes left, no eyes to see through them,
Only happy assholes plugged with pretty morals.

CONTRE

Tantes radioactives radieuses puisque c'est la seule façon
    d'être radicalement contre cette société si
    abominablement chatte.
Réceptacle des fondamentales négations, haine contre!
Ne pas donner prise. Nier.
Somptueusement.
Coït procréateur, moteur de la perpétuelle abomination!
                            Haine et tantouzeries contre!

Jusqu'à ce que vienne un homme.
Mais il ne peut pas naître de ces vagineries-là.

AGAINST

Radiant radioactive queens is the only way to stand radically
    against this appallingly pussy society.
Receptacles of fundamental negations, despising those
against!
Giving no quarter. Denying.
Sumptuously.
Procreative coitus, driving force of perpetual loathing!
                              Hatred and contra-queenery!

Until there comes one man
Of no vaginaries born.

LES AUBES

Elle va sortir, goutte gigantesque, appuyez sur ce membre.
Un reflet le parcourt: et le soleil jaillit.
Il écrit d'un jet ma joie carnassière, la première syllabe de
    mon refus.

BSM, Pointe-Pescade, 23 août 1967

DAWNS

It's about to come, gigantic globule, press on this member.
A reflection passes through it: and the sun suddenly shines.
In one spurt it spells out my carnivorous joy, first syllable of
    my rejection.

BSM, Pointe-Pescade August 23, 1967

MAIS TOI

Mais toi, Jacques, tu me parlais de la lumière avec des mots
    qui n'étaient pas une prison.
Du labyrinthe je ramène des déchets d'ailes. Ariane,
Ça fait des siècles qu'elle a crevé d'horreur
Sous les godasses, transportée par les poux, à petites étapes
Jusqu'aux fenêtres de Thésée.
O Jaaacques, avec des billes d'agate
Et des accords de saéta, tu me faisais un radeau pour l'orient.

Voilà, j'y suis
C'est la lèpre et la rage.
Mais gratte gratte, tu me dis, comme un chien.
Dessous toujours y a la rose.
La rose-des-chiens mais la rose !

BUT YOU

But you, Jacques, you spoke of light to me in words that
    were not prisons.
From the labyrinth I retrieved this wreckage of wings.
    Ariadne,
It has been centuries since horror struck her down,
Trampled, transported by lice, in small stages
Back to Theseus's windows.
Oh, Jaaacques, with cat's-eye marbles
And saeta chords, you built me a raft to sail the Orient.

But here I am
It's leprosy and rabies.
Scratch scratch, you tell me, like a dog.
A rose lies beneath.
A dog-rose perhaps, but a rose nonetheless!

TORRIDE

Faites-moi boire la mer, faites-moi boire
Votre corps contre un rocher, faites-moi
Boire les syllabes qui me replacent sur mes chevilles.
Je suis si las des mots qui nient
Ma honte ...

A travers tous vos corps, déluges glorieux, par le galbe de
    Dieu, j'arrive.
A la fenêtre les piments tintent, l'ail
Sourit. Faites-moi boire
L'orgeat glacé. Je dors
Sur votre lyre. Faites-moi boire
Jusqu'à l'aube. Faites-moi boire jusqu'aux
Os.

BSM, Pointe-Pescade, 23 août 1967

TORRID

Make me drink up the sea, make me
Drink your body against the rocks. Make me
drink the syllables that set me back on my ankles.
I am so tired of words that deny
My shame...

And I arrive through your bodies, your glorious
    outpourings, your divinely-turned legs.
At the window, hanging peppers chime and the garlic
smiles. Make me drink
Chilled orgeat. I sleep
On your lyre. Make me drink
Until dawn. Make me drink to the
Bones.

BSM, Pointe-Pescade August 23, 1967

NOIR C'EST NOIR

Et puis je sortirai vêtu de frénésie (toutes plumes dehors—
     de nostalgie peut-être)
Et vous me baiserez dans des couloirs, entre des roches
(Percussion des poubelles, shahnai des flots),
Puis vous renierez mon visage.
O rues!
Néon des lâches! néon des corrompus !
Qui es-tu ?
Oui qui suis-je?
Qui SOMMES-NOUS
Nous qui n'avons partagé que les excréments et le sperme?

BLACK IS BLACK

And then in a frenzy I'll get dressed up (flashing my
    plumage—out of nostalgia, perhaps)
And you will screw me in the halls, or between the rocks
(Trashcan percussion, shahnai of waves),
Then you will deny that you ever knew me
Oh streets!
Neon of cowardice! Neon of corruption!
Who are you?
Yes, Who am I?
And who ARE WE
Having only shared our gism and shit?

ET TANT DE PEAU

Et tant de peau quand nous cherchons
Un tunnel en griffes vers l'âme!
Le désir n'a jamais suscité que des râles
—Mais le Souffle ô vivants?

Parchemins (mes corps de Septembre),
Quand la joie dans une morsure
Condense l'espace et le temps,
Quel signe mettez-vous sous ma dent?

(L'odeur de notre mort siffle dans les glycines.)
Nous sommes nus.
Vienne la nuit
Et le soleil reprend sa chance.

Quel aveu bloque le printemps?

AND SO MUCH SKIN

And so much skin when we seek
A shaft of claws on our way to the soul!
Death-rattles are the only thing that desire has ever aroused
—But, we who live, what about the Breath?

Strips of parchment (my September bodies)
Time and space become one
In that pleasure of teeth sunk into flesh.
But what sign do you give me to bite into?

(The stench of our death whistles through the wisteria.)
We are naked.
Let the night come
And let the sun try its luck again.

Which of our confessions have kept the spring from
    coming?

UNE FOIS PLUS, JAAAA...

Jaaaaaaaaaaaacques, le vaisseau amiral et le radeau d'orient
J'ai tant rêvé qu'ils ont le délire d'Icare!
Il y a une odeur de poix en ce moment!
Moi qui n'aime que le soleil je hurle pour des nuages !

Ce n'est pas le Déluge qui m'attend
Mais un ange en deux dans mes bras
Disloqué sous sa cendre et froid
Comme les nuits où je t'appelle.

A mon genou des brisures (lettres) se forment.
Quel chant de peste se met en marche?
Quelle subtile couleur dont la vibration
Rompra mon balcon sur la mer ?

Il n'y a plus de recours, Jacques,
Ni même d'un naufrage.
Dans la bave et le chiendent
Malgré moi mon poème tend sa page.

Je voulais inventer un monde
Plus vaste que ton sourire.
Regarde, tout fout le camp, Jaaacques!
Et dans mes mains (c'est ça qui est atroce) le soleil, la terre
    continuent.

ONCE MORE, JAAAA...

Jaaaaaaaaaaaaacques, I dreamed so much of flagships and
    Oriental rafts
That they became mad as Icarus.
(Right now there's a whiff of caulk!)
I, who love only the sun, cried out for clouds!

But it's not the Flood that awaits me
It's an angel broken in two in my arms
Dismembered, covered in ashes and cold
As the nights I call out for you.

Fissures like letters form at my knee.
What dirge strikes up for the plague?
What subtle colors will quake my balcony
On the sea?

Nothing can stop it, Jacques,
Not even a shipwreck
In the slobber and switch grass.
And still, despite myself, my poem offers its page.

I wanted to imagine a world
Far wider than your smile.
Look, Jaaacques! It's all going to hell
And in my hands—and this is what makes it so terrible—
the sun and earth keep on going.

UN DERNIER RÊVE, MARGOT, AVANT LA MORT

Mais Antar va venir. J'ai toujours dit
Qu'il sortirait de mes plaies comme un étendard blanc sans
    signe
Lorsqu'un vent assez fort fera de mon corps
La mer Rouge.
Vent d'Ailleurs ou vent des Racines?
Oh qu'il ouvre en deux le poème!
Antar naîtra. Pas besoin de sa bouche pour m'envahir je
    t'aime.
Il ne restera rien du crime ni de la nuit.

ONE LAST DREAM, MARGOT, BEFORE DEATH

But Antar will come. I have always said
That he would emerge from my wounds like a white flag
    without a sign
When a rather strong wind will turn my body into
The Red Sea.
Wind from Elsewhere or Wind of Roots?
Split my poem in two!
And Antar will be born. No need for his tongue to invade
    me I love you.
Nothing will remain of the crime or the night.

HYPERPRISME BSM

Rien mais toi soleil
Planète intérieure
Père impétueux qui me gave de son stupre
Stuc
Entre les vertèbres lien–ronce
Passeport pour la nuit
Méduse sans radeau
Mémoire entre deux sexes
Vers une Méditerranée possible
Un Corps possible

Soleil griffu plus transitoire
Qu'une goutte de sperme sur ma mâchoire.

BSM, Pointe-Pescade, 25-26 1967

178

HYPERPRISM BSM

Nothing but you sunlight
Internal planet
Impetuous father who force-feeds me his squalor
Mortar
Between the link–prickly–bush vertebrae
Passport for the night
Medusa without a raft
Memory caught between one cock
And the next
Towards a potential Mediterranean
A potential Body

The clawed sun lasts no longer
Than a drop of semen on my chin.

BSM, Pointe-Pescade, August 25-26 1967

dérision et Vertige
Trouvures

…Je vivais, non déchu mais traqué.
Toute noblesse humaine étant emprisonnée
J'étais libre parmi les esclaves masqués.

Robert Desnos

derision et Vertigo
discovoids

...I lived, not demeaned but hunted down.
All human nobility having been imprisoned,
I was free amongst the masked slaves.

Robert Desnos

OS

Gratté jusqu'au signe ton corps
Roule avec le varech de flaques en rivages
Parmi les détritus et l'exclamation du mazout.
Qui chante sinon le vent brisé
Dans le caveau d'un coquillage?
Du galet à la rouille
Tout est fugace, rien ne meurt,
Tout est langage de momie.
Jeunesse continue, genêts fous de l'espace,
Même les décombres sourient!
Tes os très blancs dans l'euphorie des vagues
Charrient des matinées.

Pointe-Pescade, 3 mars 1967

BONE

Scratched down to the sign, your body
Rolls with the kelp from pools to shore
In the rubbish and the oil's exclamation.
Who sings in the seashell's cave
If not the shattered wind?
From pebbles to rust
Everything is fleeting, nothing dies,
It's all mummy language.
Youth, crazy broom of space, keep on,
Even the rubble smiles!
In the euphoria of waves, entire mornings
Are carried along by your stark white bones.

Pointe-Pescade March 3, 1967

JEUNE DÉLUGE
(K.T. d'Oran)

1

Et voici que je m'interroge sur une simple hésitation de tes
    chevilles
une mèche rebelle un mot cassé
je
traverse tes paysages—épouse répudiée
pas même nubile et déjà roue de flammes
je
m'interroge alors que le talon sur mon épaule
tu prends le départ du
feu.

2

Rien
De toi je ne sais que
le poids d'un peu d'encre à l'étal d'un libraire
et le grondement sur la rampe
des camions chargés de fûts
(Bois courbe et la lie
de l'enfance
où tu m'entraînes
O
pour ne rien
savoir.
—Je t'appellerai quand à brasses pressées
tes cuisses bleues pesant sur le poème
tu remonteras de mon corps.)
Je t'appellerai.

YOUNG DELUGE

(K.T. from Oran)

1

And here I'm wondering about the slightest hesitation of
    your ankles
an unruly strand of hair a broken word
I
cross your landscapes—repudiated wife
not yet at the age of consent and already a wheel of fire
I
wonder while with your heel on my shoulder
you take leave of the
fire.

2

Nothing
About you I know only
the weight of a little ink at the bookseller's stall
and the rumbling on the ramp
of the trucks loaded with casks
(Curved wood and the dregs
of childhood
where you lead me
Oh
to know
nothing.
—I will call you when with your blue thighs
weighing on the poem you'll rise
in hurried breaststrokes from my body.)
I will call you.

Approche de la négation.
Arrache à la pensée sa crème de tigresse.
Tire de leur purin les mots.
Ne ferme pas les yeux quand ton jumeau t'enfonce
La langue jusqu'à la lettre A.
Un déluge peut déferler
Où tu n'attendais qu'une comptine,
Et parmi le cresson
Une cinquième saison prendre d'assaut le ciel.

Pointe-Pescade, 24-26 avril 1967

Approach negation.
Rip away the tigress's cream from your thought.
Pull the words out of their watery excrement.
Don't close your eyes when your twin drives
His tongue into you until it hits the letter A.
A deluge can erupt
Where you expected just a nursery rhyme,
And among watercress
A fifth season can strike the sky.

Pointe-Pescade April 24-26 1967

NUIT VIVE II

L'ampoule au bout du fil,
Dites aux mots de revenir.

Ma main fermée sur votre sexe
Dites à l'accent circonflexe
                    de revenir.

Aux baigneurs sur la grande mer
                    de mon poème
                        de revenir.

Les vitres en hésitation
Du vitrail au verre à bouchon,
Dites aux mots de revenir.

Et toi, tes lèvres en satellite
Autour de tous mes combats, de tous mes délits,
Dis-leur de revenir, dis-leur
                    de rouler leurs galets, leurs cris.

De butor, leur sale caractère,
Leur pèlerinage des Saintes, leur Mecque, leur
            Lamentation.

Le pal au bout du fil,
Dites au père prodigue
                    de revenir,
Sur la nappe de jeter son couffin de mots, ses barreaux.

D'éblouir.
Et dans notre orgasme
                    de creuser son lit.

BRIGHT NIGHT II

Light bulb at the end of the wire,
Call the words back.

My hand held tight on your sex
Call the circumflex
            call it back

Swimmers on the vast sea
            of my poem
                    call them back.

Window panes that falter
Between stained glass and crystal stopper
Call the words back.

And you, with your lips like satellites,
Orbiting all my battles, all my crimes,
Call them back, tell them
                  to roll their stones, their cries.

Their loutish, nasty tempers,
Their pilgrimage to Saintes, to Mecca, their
        Lamentation.

Stake at the end of the wire,
Tell the prodigal father
           to come back.
To throw down on the table his cradle of words, his bars.

Tell him to dazzle.
And from our gism
           scoop out his bed.

(Mon lit ferme sur votre cri,
Dites aux mots de revenir.)

Ce que la nuit avec ses blancs
Peut faire de trous dans notre sang !

(My bed in which your cry is wrapped,
Call the words back.)

How the night with its unwritten spaces
Can make in our blood such vacant places!

LÉGENDE

Vous avez vu le soleil,
D'abord,
Avec ses cinq doigts
Tout le bleu de la mer
Et le plaisir des tentes. Vous avez vu
L'éblouissante paresse (le sommeil et la joie),
Le loisir des mots, la confiance.
Vous avez vu
Le chardon —mais sur un horizon si vaste !
Et dans ces draps
Jamais la mort
Mais un corps jeune,
Un bec de plume.

Vous avez vu le combat, le refus,
Mais jamais dans la plaie ce roulement de dunes,
Dieu comme une miette refusée, l'homme
Dans son entreprise, toujours aux prises avec ses excréments.

Vous avez vu le chant,
L'éjaculation,
La rose.

Mais toi solitude
Ton oursin de fer
Ils ne l'ont pas vu
Coincé dans mes vers.

Alger-Reclus, 6 mai 1970

LEGEND

You saw the sun,
First
With its five fingers
All the blue of the sea
And the pleasure of the tents. You saw
The dazzling idleness (sleep and joy),
The leisure of words, trust.
You saw
The thistle—but on such a vast horizon!
And in these sheets
Never death
But a young body,
With a quill point.

You saw the battle, the rejection
But never in the wound these rumbling dunes,
God like a rejected crumb, man
In his undertakings, always in the grips with his excrement.

You saw the song,
The ejaculation,
The rose.

But they did not see
You, solitude, with
Your iron sea urchin
Wedged in my verse.

Algiers-Reclus May 6, 1970

LAURIERS DU FIGUIER

Viens, amer.
A travers les roseaux
Ton estime rose
M'est plus qu'un répit.
Peut-être un accroc, l'accès
A la Déchirure
Au-delà de laquelle tout redevient naissance.

★

Je vais sur vos hanches, Colomb, vers de fabuleuses contrées.
Rites, danses, trésors, fantastiquement lumineux et nus
    m'acquiescent.
En toi je me réjouis, en toi mon ascèse est un feu de camp.
Erige-toi, colonne aztèque, fournaise de joie, que chante
La caravelle! Batailles de plumes, jets
Radieux, tout mon corps sur toi se referme.

Cormonaute!
Sur ton slip déjà tournoient les mouettes.
Retire-le! Voici les Indes! O
Mon amour!
(Mais en moi demeure je ne sais quelle appréhension de
    Cortez ...)

★

Conquérant me voici soumis par ma conquête,
Rendu aux dieux barbares,
Dépossédé.
Et je deviens tout simplement le géographe
Vers cette cataracte où ton innocence m'entraîne,

FIGUIER'S LAURELS

Come, bitter.
Through the reeds
Arose your erotic respect
More for me than a respite.
Like a snag, perhaps, the access
To the Fissure
Beyond which everything becomes a birth again.

★

I sail on your hips, Columbus, towards fabulous lands
Fantastically luminous and naked rites, dances and treasures
    nod to me their approval.
Within you I am thrilled, within you my austerity becomes
    a bonfire.
Raise yourself up, Aztec column, blaze of joy, of whom the caravel
Sings! Battle of feathers, radiant
Jets, my whole body closes over you.

Anatonaut!
The sea gulls already are circling your Speedo.
Take it off! There are the Indies! Oh
My love!
(But within me remains some foreboding of Cortez...)

★

I am the conqueror and here I am enslaved by my conquest,
Captive to the barbarian gods,
Dispossessed.
I have become merely the geographer
Of the waterfall where your innocence drags me,

195

L'explorateur émerveillé du fleuve et de la flore,
Célébrant en cette libation je ne sais déjà quel rite funèbre.

★

Je te suce et tu cries: «Réjouis-moi!»
Comme si je ne sais de quel abîme il fallait tirer ce pétrole.

★

Je croyais n'avoir que deux bras, deux jambes, un sexe,
Tu me fais retrouver le dragon lacté
Aux mille membres, les arabesques de mes sens.
Une autre parole dont le gémissement est l'inflexion première.
Syllabes sauvages et corps sauvage.
Et m'ayant donné l'Amérique tu te retires dans tes temples.

★

Tu es la perpétuelle présence.
Il ne fallait pas me donner accès au plaisir.
Mémoire, imagination—et la main!
Avec moi tu restes!

(Et là nous refaisons le cours des fleuves, la
Forme des arbres, les bêtes
Fastueuses.
Sous mes doigts nous renaissons dans une unité si parfaite
Que la colonne s'écroule—et d'un cri je touche à la mort.)

★

Ta lyre et ta toison,
Tes dents où je pirogue,
Tes cuisses où l'avenir s'écrit en jeux poignants.

196

The explorer filled with wonder by the river and the flora,
Celebrating in this libation who-knows-what funereal rite.

★

I suck and you cry: "Thrill me!"
As if this oil had to be extracted from who-knows-what abyss.

★

I thought I had only two arms, two legs, one sex,
You have allowed me to rediscover the thousand-leggèd
Milky dragon, the arabesques of my senses.
Another form of speech whose moan is the original inflection.
Savage syllables and savage body.
And having given me America you withdraw into your temples.

★

You are the presence everlasting.
You shouldn't have given me access to such pleasure.
Memory, imagination—and the hand!
You have stayed with me!

(And there we retrace the rivers' course, the
Shape of the trees, the magnificent
Animals.
Under my touch we are reborn in a unity so perfect
The column collapses—and with a cry I close on death.)

★

Your lyre and your fleece
Your teeth where I canoe
Your thighs where the future is written in poignant play.

197

La stimulation de la tempête, la tempête, l'oubli de la
    tempête.
Un mot à peine, idiot, pour annoncer plaisir et mort, merci.
Et tes pupilles qui regagnent leur planète.
Tu me laisses seul avec mon angoissante joie —l'impact des
    soucoupes volantes.

(Retourner aux laboratoires.
Recomposer ta lyre et ta toison.
Je n'ai d'écriture que palpable.
Corpoème, échec triomphant!)

                        ★

Ta salive et ton sperme,
Ce corps que tu as embelli de tes traces,
Ta sueur, mon zodiaque fou,
Légende périssable, de ce Tassili
Ne restera-t-il que mes mots?

                        ★

O mes milliers d'adolescents
Je te tutoie veux-tu?
De Morgeat ou de Tamadecht,
De Paris ou de Barcelone.
De Bab-el-Oued ou de Moscou
(Et vous mes pèlerins de Saint-Jacques où Nerval aspire
La ténèbre sur vos genoux).
Te tutoie car tu es
Dans le futile éclair de tes dents et des cuisses
Non le dragon de mes délices
Mais l'unique colombe et ma seule vertu.
(Et vous mes estivants, donateurs sous les tentes
Du prénom de chaque vague,

198

The stimulation of the tempest, the tempest, the oblivion of
     the tempest.
Barely a word, a meaningless word announcing pleasure and
     death, thanks.
And your eyes return to their planet.
You leave me alone with my agonizing joy—the impact of
     flying saucers.

(To return to the laboratories.
To reconstitute your lyre and your fleece.
I have only the palpable act of writing.
Corpoem, triumphant failure!)

★

Your saliva and your sperm,
This body that you have embellished with your tracks,
Your sweat, my mad zodiac,
Perishable legend, will only my words remain
Of this Tassili?

★

Oh my thousands of boys
Do you mind if I speak to you as a friend?
From Morgeat or Tamadecht,
From Paris or Barcelona.
From Bab-el-Oued or Moscow
(And you my pilgrims on your knees from Santiago de
     Compostela where Nerval breathes in the darkness.)
Speak to you as a friend for you are
In the futile flash of your teeth and your thighs
Not the dragon of my delights
But the lone dove and my sole virtue.
(And you my summer tourists, my donors under the tents
With the first name of each wave

199

Du soleil de chaque plaie,
Peut-être dans ces délires du Figuier une Autre Beauté s'est-
    elle mise en route?)

★

Amer,
Mais du moins tes feuilles ne sont pas coupantes.
Et les adolescents sur la plage portent des maillots à tes
    couleurs.
Quand les roseaux frémissent
Ton rose vient mêler à notre encre
Son insolence et sa pudeur.
Ici,
Aujourd'hui encore,
Sous les quolibets et les lois,
Quinquet assailli et soleil,
Dans la pauvreté, la saillie, l'espace,
Sous ta vigie,
Je règne.

Le Figuier, 10-11 août 1970

With the sun of each wound,
Perhaps in the delirium of Figuier has
Another Beauty been set in motion?)

★

Bitter,
But at least your leaves don't cut me.
The boys on the beach wear trunks in your colors.
When the reeds tremble
Your rosy hue mixes into our ink
Its impertinence and modesty.
Here
Still today
Subjected to the jeers and laws,
Bull's eye lanterns under attack and sun,
In this poverty, this barb, this space
With you at your lookout.
I rule.

Le Figuier, August 10-11, 1970

RÉDA-DU-RIVAGE

Je t'apporterai un collier de nacres
Il faut vingt jours pour en rassembler un
Mais tous les crépuscules viendront ensuite sur ta poitrine
    pour éclairer ma joie
Sur ton épaule gauche la lune
Sur ta droite le soleil
Entre deux aubes le poème
Parce que je t'aime j'écris
Du fond des cataractes j'annonce la source.

RÉDA-OF-THE·SHORE

I will bring you a necklace of mother-of-pearl
One you need twenty days to assemble
But then on your chest each dusk will come to shed light
   on my joy
On your left shoulder the moon
On your right the sun
Between the two dawns the poem
Because I love you I write
And from deep within the waterfall I foretell the source.

ABDALLAH RIMBAUD
(ABDOH RINBO)

à Serge Tamagnot

A Tipasa soudain me revient du Harar
Le sceau,
L'héritage de Djami,
Ton cri lorsqu'il—ou ce silencespace—te pénétrait.
Me vient
Ton nom qui n'était plus Arthur.
Enfin
Nommé! Et Serviteur.
De plein consentement. Cerclé de sable et d'épineuses.
Puis le silence.
(Et cet ivrogne en toi sans fin qui bouge,
Secoue ses brumes, son clavecin,
Ses oiseaux dans la nuit,
Tandis que Djami t'ouvre et t'inonde te boit
T'accouche.)
Tout un désert pour lit.
La panoplie de bleu, d'urine et d'or massif.
A Tipasa tandis
Que Brahim et Samir font de cette confusion de muscles,
    d'os, de nerfs,
Un corps,
Me revient ton prénom qui refuse le Cycle
Augure
   Insoumis
Vers Ailleurs.

Tipasa, 25 septembre 1970

204

ABDALLAH RIMBAUD
(ABDOH RINBO)

To Serge Tamagnot

In Tipasa it suddenly comes back to me,
the seal, Djami's legacy,
all the way from Harrar,
Your cry when he—or that silencespace—penetrated you.
Your name which was no longer Arthur
Comes to me.
Finally
Named! And Servant
Consenting completely. Encircled by sand and prickly
    plants.
Then silence.
(And the drunk within you that never stops moving,
Shakes off his stupor, his harpsichord,
His birds in the night,
As Djami opens you, floods you, drinks you
Delivers you.)
An entire desert for a bed.
The whole spectrum of blue, urine and solid gold.
In Tipasa as
Brahim and Samir produce from this confusion of muscles,
    bones and nerves,
A body,
Your first name comes back to me rejecting the
Oracle Cycle
      Insubordinate
Towards Elsewhere.

Tipasa, September 25, 1970

205

ODE À CERNUDA

Maudite la langue que je parle.
Maudit mon pays et maudit mon peuple.
Maudite cette seconde où marqué de la pierre marginale
J'émergeais ici. O maudit
Ce qui fait ma gloire et ma force.

Vers ce torse
Svelte et sombre
Ebloui sans rature
Espace du désir
Vers ces cuisses
Vulnérables et solennelles
(Si l'on me dresse un arc
Que ce soit celui-là!)
Vers ces lèvres
Gâchées par le mot
Et que le baiser sauve
Espace du désir
Don Luis
Une fois de plus
Le poème ose et risque.

Leurs quolibets et les graillons du rire
S'abattent sur le marbre en feu—rien ne les brûle,
Ils ont la vulgarité ignifuge.
(Et la bêtise aussi est un phénix, nous ne le savions pas.)

Mais nous avançons vers la forme première
(«...Lorsque la mer évidente,
Sous l'irréfutable soleil de midi,
Suspendait mon corps
Dans cette abdication de l'homme devant son dieu...»)

ODE TO CERNUDA

Cursèd be the language I speak.
Cursèd be my country and my people.
Cursèd be this second when, marked by the marginal stone,
I emerged here. O cursèd be
What gave me fame and strength.

Towards that torso
Slim and dark
Dazzled with no revisions
Space of desire
Towards those thighs
Vulnerable and solemn
(If they build me an ark
May it be that one!)
Towards those lips
Ruined by the word
And that are saved by the kiss
Space of desire
Don Luis
Once more
The poem dares and risks.

Their jibes and laughter's spit
Pour down in flames on the marble—nothing burns them,
Their vulgarity is fire-proof
(And—we didn't know this— stupidity is a phoenix, as well.)

But we advance towards the original form
("...When the evident sea,
Under the irrefutable noon sun,
Suspended my body
In this abdication of man before his god...")

Toujours au plus aigu de la toison et de l'orage,
Au périlleux du mot. Anéantie, l'image
Tourbillonne et nous recompose l'univers. Respirable.
Nos poumons deviennent le Livre. Le souffle adolescent
     écrit.
Jamais plus que dans ces pupilles notre visage rebelle avoue
Son royaume et sa confusion. Pupilles planète mon exil
Ma soucoupe volante mon île ma transmutation.

Ce serait si simple...Franchi le rempart, les glaires
Nous traquent et de nouveau reprennent les journées
     visqueuses,
La phrase répressive, familles religions lois.
De nouveau du soleil ils font un oursin de métal
Qu'ils frottent sur nos lèvres—jusqu'à l'urine.

Maudite ma langue nourrice de discorde.
Maudit mon pays qui ne sait embrasser que pour jeter son
     pus.
Mais jamais le poème—Qu'il reste
Sur la mer cet adolescent nu !

Comme l'autre à Médine,
Nous fuyons et pourtant chaque pas décrassé nous ramène
A notre peuple.
Maudit lui aussi qui refuse son rêve !
Pourtant c'est d'entre lui que montent
Cette vérité—malgré ses fouets—qui m'accorde au
     monde,
Ces corps neufs, purs et beaux.
D'entre lui ces élans qui sont réconciliation et lumière,
De son sable l'agave nu que je préfère à tous les arbres,
Et le signe de calcination.
Pourtant il n'est pour moi ni patrie ni poème.
Hors de cette rocaille refuge du scorpion.

Always at the height of fleece and storm,
At the word's most perilous. Annihilated, the image
Swirls and reassembles the universe for us. Breathable.
Our lungs become the Book. The adolescent breath writes.
Never more than in those eyes does our rebellious
    expression confess
Its domain and its confusion. Eyes planet my exile
My flying saucer my island my transmutation.

It would be so simple...Having scaled the rampart, the glair
Hunts us down and once more begin the viscous days,
The repressive words, families religions laws.
Once more they make a metal urchin of the sun
That they rub on our lips until they strike urine

Cursèd by my wet nurse's tongue of discord.
Cursèd be my country which only kisses to throw off its
    pus.
But never the poem—Let it remain
That naked youth on the sea!

Like the other one at Medina
We flee and yet each step scrubbed clean brings us back
To our people.
Cursèd be the one who also rejects their dream!
And yet it is from within the people that
This truth rises—despite its whip—that brings me into
    harmony with the world.
These new bodies, pure and beautiful.
Those impulses within them bring reconciliation and light,
From their sand the naked agave that I prefer above all trees,
And the mark of calcination.
And yet for me there is no homeland or poem
Apart from this stony scorpion's refuge.

J'avancerai.
Si différent de toi, si proche,
Grand frère opaque, mercure, rosée sur le chardon.
Jamais miroir n'a rendu plus profond
Le Cerne
Et du laurier les ordalies féroces.
Mais, ô Cernuda, dans ces accrocs, ces poches, que d'étoiles à
l'abandon ...

Tipasa, 25 septembre 1970

210

I will move foward.
So different from you, so close,
Impenetrable older brother, mercury, dew on the thistle.
Never before has a mirror made
Cerne
And the laurel's ordeals so fearsome.
But, oh Cernuda, in these snags and these pockets, how
    many untended stars.

Tipasa, September 25, 1970

PARDON À RENÉ CHAR

mon maître, tandis que je coule
vers Armand Sully Prudhomme

Un grand poète se remarque à la quantité
de pages insignifiantes qu'il n'écrit pas. Il a
toutes les rues de la vie oublieuse pour distribuer
ses moyennes aumônes et cracher le
petit sang dont il ne meurt pas.

R.C.

1

Cette écritoire, cette fresque,
Pour tout dire ce drap sale,
Fallait-il en faire la voile
De mon radeau amiral ?

Et cette plaie mauresque
Fallait-il en faire un blason
Au lieu d'aller à l'hôpital
Guérir ou presque?

Fallait-il ouvrir mes poubelles
Avec ces morceaux de cervelle
Plus ou moins blancs

Et ces syllabes qui se traînent
Comme des chiennes
Vers l'horizon ?

212

APOLOGY TO RENÉ CHAR

*my teacher, as I sink down
towards Armand Sully Prudhomme*

*A great poet stands out by the amount
of insignificant pages that he does not write. He has
all the streets of this forgetful life on which to distribute
his average gifts of charity and to spit his
bit of blood that doesn't kill him.*

R.C.

1

This writing case, these epic tales
In honesty this dirty sheet
Should I have made them into sails
for my flagship fleet?

Should I have turned into a blazon
This Moorish laceration
Instead of going to the clinic
To heal or not quite?

Should I take my trash from under wraps
With its cerebellum scraps
That are more or less white?

And these syllables crawling round
Like hounds
Towards the horizon?

213

La colère et le tact,
Cet éclair dans un bol,
Ce volcan tenu exact,
Cet équateur dans ce pôle.

Tout Rimbaud, tout Antonin
Dans l'aphorisme sans transe.
Et moi dans tout mon purin:
« Qu'est-ce que René Char en pense? »

Ai-je truqué le mystère
Douce poésie malade?
Pourra-t-il dans cette terre
Encore pousser un arbre?

C'est bien mauvais (oui Robert),
Certains disent que ça sent,
Il aurait suffi pourtant
D'ouvrir le balcon sur la mer...

J'habite une cave.

3

Qu'es-tu, arbre à la renverse,
Racine moelle et sang
De l'éclair arborescent?

Silence.

2

Anger and tact
That lightning in a bowl,
That volcano kept on track
That equator at this pole

All Antonin and all Rimbaud
In untrancelatable bons mots
And me in all my liquid shit
"What does René think of it?"

Did I fake the mystery
Sweet and sickly poetry?
Is there possibility
In this earth to grow a tree?

Yes, Robert, this is real bad stuff
Some say it stinks, and opening
the balcony on the sea
Would have been quite good enough...

I live in a cave.

3

What are you, fallen tree,
Root marrow and blood
Of the arborescent lightning bolt?

4

Silence

ORDRE II

Quand j'aurai retiré mon poète
Mon pédé ma barbe mon bâtard
Mon algérien mon sommeil
Mon soleil (slip minimum) mon
Bavardage ma mer,
Dévêtu comme un pape sur le seuil de Dieu,
Nu
Comme un empereur pour le sacre,
(Ouvrier sous la douche)
—mon mendigot—,
Vous me verrez.
Avec une poitrine capable d'accueillir l'espérance et l'espace.
Des épaules pour le temps
Des poumons un cœur réguliers
Pour une marche souple
Parmi la vigoureuse tendresse du matin
(Genou intact, Rimbaud sauvé),
Vous m'aimerez.
En attendant, avec tous ces mots de nylon,
Je transpire et je feins.

Alger, 17 octobre 1970

ORDER II

When I will have stripped away my poet
My fag my beard my bastard
My Algerian my sleep
My sun (the skimpiest bathing suit) my
Chattiness my sea,
When I'm undressed like a pope on God's threshold
Naked
Like an emperor awaiting anointment,
(Worker in the shower)
—my vagrant—
You will see me.
With a chest that can take in hope and space.
Shoulders for time
Steady lungs and heart
For a fluid motion
Through the vigorous affection of the morning
(Knee intact, Rimbaud saved),
You will love me.
Meanwhile, I sweat and feign
with all these nylon words.

Algiers, October 17th, 1970

217

RACAILLE ARDENTE
(Préface à vaincre II)

...pas un poème—le constat...

Description d'un cauchemar:

«J'ai vu ce pays se défaire
Avant même de s'être fait.
Lâcheté, paresse, délation,
Corruption, intrusion constante,
Dénigrement systématique, méchanceté, vulgarité
—Les pires pieds-noirs cent fois battus!
J'ai vu la joie, l'honneur, la beauté n'être plus
Qu'un masque délavé sur la plus lamentable racaille.
Avant même de prendre corps
Ici l'âme s'est écroulée.
Voyez ces morts vivants à l'abjecte arrogance!
Pays de zombies, de fantômes,
Enfants aigris, caillés dès le lait maternel.
L'Algérie fut, sera peut-être...
Cet immense cloaque pavoisé c'est quoi?

Et je t'avais chanté ô peuple!
Cafards, roquets, sous-hommes entre les mains de quelle maffia?
Où sont les regards? Où les couilles?
Qui ose affronter un ragot?
Veulerie, mensonge et la trouille
Géante au centre du drapeau.
Mécaniques cassées sans pièces de rechange,
Pets surgonflés d'europes asthmatiques et de marmaillantes
    zaouïas,
Voyez-les parader comme des rots de rats

FERVENT RABBLE
(Preface to Conquer II)

...not a poem—an affidavit

Description of a nightmare:

"I saw this country come apart
Before it even came together.
Baseness, indolence, denunciation,
Corruption, constant intrusion
Systematic denigration, spite, vulgarity
— The worst pieds-noirs beaten a hundred times!
I saw joy, honor, beauty, become no more than a faded mask
   worn by the most appalling rabble.
Here, even before taking shape
The soul collapsed.
See the living dead with their abject arrogance!
Nation of zombies, of ghosts
Of embittered children, curdled since their first taste of
   mother's milk.
Algeria was, will be perhaps...
What's this vast festooned cesspool?

And I had sung your praises oh, people!
Roaches, curs, subhumans in the hands of what gangsters?
Where are the penetrating looks? The balls?
Who dares confront slander?
Spinelessness, lies and immense fear
Smack in the middle of the flag.
Broken machinery without spare parts,
Bloated farts from asthmatic europes
And punk-producing zaouias
See them parade about like rat's burps

Parmi leurs détritus et leurs maigres vitrines.

Ça mon peuple, ah que non! Ce vil tresseur de corde
Prêt à rependre Ben M'Hidi?
Cette crasse érigée en plastron de discorde,
Ce Judas sans parole qui cent fois se trahit?

Je l'ai chanté pourtant, mais c'était d'autres hommes.
Des hommes simplement dressés comme un seul homme
Pour apporter le jour où serpentait la nuit.
Oh taisez-vous mon sang bientôt voici Novembre
Qui ne sera qu'un mois d'ordures et de pluies.»

Alger-Reclus, 26 septembre 1971

Comment et pourquoi, en 1971, le poète qui avait écrit:
«J'ai vu le peuple le plus beau de la terre
Sourire au fruit et le fruit se donner.»
a-t-il pu se laisser aller à ce terrible «reportage»? Jeunes gens de
l'avenir, creusez, creusez …
Pour conjurer l'atroce vision, je ressors cette carte postale de
l'Indépendance:

SOLEIL DE NOVEMBRE

Ce que j'ai vu en arrivant dans ma patrie ce sont les yeux.
La Révolution a donné un regard à ce peuple.
Beauté de nos gosses à l'orée du jour!
Quelle certitude et pour nous tous quel pacte!
Voilà un devoir tout tracé: le bonheur de l'Homme à
    restituer aux hommes. Le bonheur, c'est-à-dire : le pain,
    le toit, le travail, l'instruction.

220

Through their garbage and their near–empty shop windows.

That? My people?—No, not at all! The vile rope braider
Again ready to hang Ben M'Hidi?
That filth raised high like a breast plate of discord,
That Judas who doesn't keep his word and betrays himself a
    hundred times?

Yet I once sung its praises, but for other men.
Men standing simply as a single man
To provide daylight where night meanders.
Oh, my blood be quiet for soon it will be November
And November will be merely a month of rubbish and rain."

Algiers-Reclus, September 26 1971

How and why could the poet who had written:
"I saw the most beautiful people on earth
Smile at the fruit, and the fruit give itself up to them."[1]
*Have gone as far as this horrible "report" in 1971? Young people of
    the future, dig, dig...*
*To ward off this atrocious vision, I take out once more this post card
    from the time of Independence:*

NOVEMBER SUN[2]

When I arrived back in my homeland what I saw were the
    eyes.
The Revolution had given the people a way of looking.
Our children so beautiful at the edge of the day!
What certainty and all of us in such accord!

1 Cited from Sénac's earlier poem "Citizens of Beauty"
2 Following independence on November 1, 1962, this poem was published as a
post card in Algeria in the "Poésie sur tous les fronts" series.

Soleil d'une impitoyable franchise.

Soleil dans le regard de tous!
J'avais rêvé. Ce peuple est plus grand que mon rêve.
Les plus beaux livres de la Révolution sont les murs de ma
ville.
«Nous ferons de l'Algérie le chantier de l'énergie populaire.»
Au-delà du cœur brisé.
Unis, nous construirons ensemble la Maison du Peuple Eveillé.

Alger, 10 novembre 1962

Duty that's all laid out: Man's happiness to be restored
   to men. Happiness, in other words: a roof, bread, work,
   education.
A ruthless, straightforward sun.
The Sun's fire in everyone's eyes!
I had dreamed. The people are greater than my dream.
The Revolution's most beautiful books are the walls of my
   city.
"We will make Algeria the construction site of the people's
energy."
Beyond the broken heart.
As one, we will build the House of the People Awakened.

Algiers, November 10, 1962

WILDE, LORCA, ET PUIS...

L'heure est venue pour vous de m'abattre, de tuer
En moi votre propre liberté, de nier
La fête qui vous obsède. Soleil frappé, des années saccagées
Remontera
Mon CORPS.

Alger, 15 octobre 1971

WILDE, LORCA AND THEN...

The time has come for you to slaughter me, to kill
In me your own liberty, to deny
The celebration obsessed you. The stricken sun, years of
    devastation
Will lift up
My BODY.

Algiers, October 15th 1971

CETTE VILLE

à Farahnaz, pour son premier anniversaire

A ce qu'ils apportent la joie
la confiance
l'élan
vous les reconnaissez

«Ces militants», 1962.

Dans cette ville
On ne sort plus.
Les rats crèvent
Sous le cœur

★

Les oranges sont petites,
Les pommes de terre rares.
Baisers interdits,
Mosquées grasses.

★

Larmes de paysans
Pour quelle récolte?
Soc
Pour quelle rouille?
Pied nu
Pour quel sillon?

THIS CITY

To Farahnaz for her first birthday

> *You recognize them*
> *by their way of bringing joy*
> *trust*
> *energy.*

"These militants", 1962[1]

In this city
We no longer go out.
Rats are dying
Beneath the heart.

★

The oranges are small,
The potatoes rare.
Kisses forbidden,
Mosques plump.

★

Peasant tears
For what harvest?
Plowshare
For what rust?
Bare foot
For what furrow?

---

1 From Sénac's poem from "Aux Héros Purs", a collection of two poems, distributed to all the members of the Algerian National Assembly in 1962.

★

Les mots eux-mêmes ont froid.

★

Une ville habitée par les hommes.
Les femmes se voilent.
Les enfants ruminent des glaires.

★

Adolescents
Masqués de croupi.

★

Silence et pus.
Culture de déchets.

★

Culture de plastrons.
Cris et pus.

★

Famines, tabous
Et poèmes de classe
(De livres de classes).

★

Les murs peuvent se dégrader,
Mais ces regards,

228

*

The words themselves are cold.

*

A city inhabited by men.
The women wearing veils.
The children chewing snot.

*

Adolescents
Masked in rot

*

Silence and pus
Culture of waste matter.

*

Culture of swagger
Cries and pus

*

Famines, taboos
And grade school poems
(From grade school books).

*

The walls can crumble,
But those stares

Cette conscience?
Bâtir le futur avec quoi?

★

Sur la rogne, la crasse et la vulgarité,
Que fonderez-vous, ministres?
Sur ce tapage quel chant?
Sur ces tessons quelle cité?
Nationalisme avare, religion, race,
Haine du différent:
J'imagine de longs cortèges hagards vers des crématoires vert
    et blanc.

★

Pour l'instant,
Des bureaux-crématoires.

★

Héros purs.
De boue
Non plus debout?

★

Les mots font mal.
Rire de crin.

★

Dans cette ville
La jeunesse est un crime,
L'intelligence est un crime,
La beauté est un crime.

That conscience?
Build the future with what?

★

What will you establish, ministers,
On anger, filth and crudeness?
What song on this din?
What city on these shards of glass?
Stingy nationalism, religion, race,
Hatred of difference
I imagine long crazed corteges rolling towards
Green and white crematoria.

★

For now,
Crematory offices.

★

Pure heroes
Of mud
And feet of clay?

★

Words hurt
Horsehair laughter.

★

In this city
Youth is a crime,
Intelligence is a crime,
Beauty is a crime.

La médiocrité est la seule loi.
Poésie battue jusqu'au sang.

★

Dépendre Ben M'Hidi
De chaque seuil.
Jeter la corde et rendre
Au sourire son peuple.

★

Couples, je vous salue
Sur les plages futures!

★

Dans cette ville
On ne se parle plus,
On se ment.

On ne se regarde plus,
On s'épie.

On a peur.

★

On avance avec
Dans les cicatrices
Des étoiles de délation.

★

Dans cette ville
On ne t'invite pas.

232

Mediocrity is the only law.
Poetry beaten until it bleeds.

★

Take Ben M'Hidi down
From every doorway.
Throw away the rope and return
Their lost smiles to the people.

★

Couples I salute you
On future beaches!

★

In this city
We no longer talk to each other,
We lie to each other.

We don't look at each other.
We spy on each other.

We are scared.

★

We move forward with
Denouncing stars
In our scars.

★

In this city
People don't invite you.

Le soleil,
La mer,
Redents intacts.

Le saccage.

Poitrine adolescente,
Rempart,
Ne vieillis pas.
Fête pure,
Ne cède pas.
Dure
Pour tous.
Augure.

Dans cette ville,
Farahnaz lève le doigt—pas plus gros qu'une datte—
Ignore les rats, découvre
Les bivouacs du ciel
Et s'émerveille.

Alger, 18 octobre 1971

★

The sun,
The sea,
Toothing intact.

Wanton destruction.

Adolescent chest,
Rampart
Don't get old.
Pure celebration
Don't yield
Resist
For all.
Prophet

★

In this city
Farahnaz raises a finger—no bigger than a date—
Ignores the rats, discovers
The bivouacs of the sky
And marvels.

Algiers, October 18th, 1971

235

Plaques

Plaques

PLAQUES DU 24 MAI 1973

«J'ai fait ce que j'ai pu, mais tout a été vain,
aujourd'hui je suis las—pardonnez-moi—très las.
Ne m'interrogez plus: chantez face au patio...»

Gabriel Celaya

S'il me fallait fumer encore une cigarette
Avant de m'enfermer dans la froide couverture du départ,
Vous assommer encore de mes métaphores ivres
Et une dernière fois tenir bon avec vous pour que la clairière
    ne soit pas souillée
—Préserver la chance de l'ombre, la chance de la lumière, le
    nid, le chant,
Quand les ordures nous envahissent—, s'il me fallait
Interroger encore votre regard et vos hésitations,
Le verbe inquiet de sa racine, méfiant de sa sève,
Et l'ombre qui vous mord à l'heure où le paysan passe
Une fois (de plus) sa main cassée sur son front las,
S'il me fallait répondre avant de prendre congé
A tant d'amour, à tant de haine, de fidélités éclairantes, de
    lâchetés, de trahisons, s'il me fallait
Répondre du soleil et de ma langue, du mal, du bien
    accumulés,
En ma gerbe à peine bonne à fertiliser les saisons avares,
O jeunes poètes, je n'éclaterais pas du rire de l'abandon,
Je n'aurais même pas l'audace de sourire—tout
Fut si vain. Mais s'il fallait, coûte que coûte, rendre
Un mot—tout est toujours pris, tout violé, ô langage!—,
Je vous dirais encore une fois: «Dormir»,

PLAQUES FROM MAY 24, 1973

I did what I could but it was all for nothing,
today I am weary—please excuse me—very weary.
Don't ask me any more questions: sing facing the patio.

Gabriel Celaya

If I had to smoke one more cigarette
Before shutting myself up in the cold blanket of departure,
Boring you stiff once more with my drunken metaphors
And standing firm with you for one last time so that the
    forest clearing isn't trashed
—When we are overrun by rubbish
Preserving the shadow's chances, the light's chances, the nest,
    the song,
—if I had, once more, to question your gaze and your
    hesitations,
The words worried about their roots, suspicious of their vigor,
And the shadow that bites at you as the peasant passes by
His broken hand once more on his weary brow,
If I had to answer so much love, so much hatred, such
    enlightening loyalty, baseness, betrayal before taking
    leave, if I had to
Answer for the sun and my language, for the evil and the good
That have collected
In my wreath that is fit only to make stingy seasons fertile,
Oh, young poets, I would not burst out in the laughter of
    abandonment,
I wouldn't even have the nerve to smile—it was all for
nothing. But if I had to speak, at all costs,
One word—Oh language! Everything taken, everything violated—

239

Le corps encor tout plein de la réalité cognante.
Je n'ai jamais écrit que pour qu'un peu
De sommeil soit possible.
Pour tous.

Alger-Reclus
Jeudi 24 mai 1973, 6 h 45 matin

Then once more I would say: "Sleep,"
The body still saturated with bruising reality.
I only wrote so that a little bit of sleep would be possible.
For all.

Algiers-Reclus
Thursday May 24, 1973, 6:45 A.M.

LE SAGE LE FOL ORGUEIL
OU LA BONTÉ OU LE VENIN

Je colle chaque matin
Un poème à ma porte.
Qui le prend?
Les gosses du quartier?
La concierge?
Ma voisine (la Tunisienne ou celle d'Hennaya)?
Un flic?
(La bourrique d'Esposito si elle était là?)

J'ai donné comme ça des tas de recueils.
Sans garder le double.

Alger-Reclus
Jeudi 24 mai 1973, 8 h 45 matin

THE WISEMAN THE MAD PRIDE
OR GOOD OR VENOM

Every morning I tape
A poem to my door.
Who swipes it?
The neighborhood kids?
The concierge?
My neighbor (the woman from Tunisia or the one from Hennaya)?
A cop?
(If it were here, Esposito's donkey?)

In this way I've given out volumes of poems.
And not saved a single one.

Thursday, May 24th, 1973, 8:45 AM

AVEC TOUT ÇA

Avec tout ça je fais du vent,
Des petites brises, des courants
D'air vague.

Qu'on verlainise ou qu'on charrie,
Poètes à la démence aiguë,
On drague

Un mot par-là un mot par-ci,
Pour ne pas crever on divague.

On fait des océans de nôs,
Spongieuse, la mort nous laisse nos
vagues.

Alger-Reclus
Jeudi 24 mai 1973, 19 h 30

WITH ALL THIS

With all this I make a breeze.
Little winds and jet streams
Accrue.

We may verlanize or butchar
As poets with dementia
We cruise.

One word here, there another
So we don't croak we mutter
And rave.

We make oceans out of hours
Spongy death leaves us our
Waves.

Algiers-Reclus
Thursday, May 24th, 1973 , 7:30 PM

CIRCULATION

Le temps qu'elle mettra pour arriver au Centre,
Ça n'est plus bien longtemps.
Pour le moment elle hante
Les coins ardents.
Elle met des odeurs dans la bouche,
Des au revoir.
Certaines nuits elle vous touche
Comme un miroir.
Elle est soigneuse et magistrate,
Elle a son temps.
Elle a son allure et ses strates
Et ses micas éblouissants.
Dame de toutes mes aubaines
Et de mes ports,
Elle est ma colonne et ma gaine.
Bonjour la Mort !

Alger-Reclus
Jeudi 24 mai 1973, 19 h 45

CIRCULATION

The time she'll take to make the jaunt
To town is not much longer
For now she has begun to haunt
The ardent corner
In your mouth some sweet adieux
She places with an odor
And then some nights she touches you
Like a mirror
She is a judge with diligence
She also has her time.
She has her strata and elegance
Her brilliant micas shine.
My woman of opportunity
My backbone and my debt
She's my port onto the sea,
Hello, Death!

Algiers-Reclus
Thursday May 24th, 1973, 7:45 PM

LETTRE POUR ELLE

Quand vous viendrez Madame Mort
Il faudra enlever ce mors
Qui reste
Et porter à Monsieur Jésus
Ce qui dure de tout mon jus
Un zeste.

Le mot pour ne pas renoncer
Que je laisse à tous mes aimés
Si lestes
Jaune éclatant comme mon cœur
Le soleil le citron la peur
La peste.

LETTER FOR HER

When you arrive, Mrs. Death,
You'll have to take away what's left,
This horse's bit
And bring to Mr. Jesus
What remains of all my juices
A zest.

The word so as not to surrender
That I bequeath to my befrienders
So just
Bright yellow like my heart, so dear,
The sun the lemon fear
The Pest.

Pour une terre possible

For a Possible Land

A ALBERT CAMUS QUI ME TRAITAIT D'ÉGORGEUR

Moi, dit le Poète
mes mains tourbillonnent dans la vase
à l'affût des astres éteints.
Y a-t-il un autre moyen
de les ramener à la surface,
d'en faire des diamants,
de rayer les vitres opaques?

Qui nous lavera, dit le Maître de l'Absolu
quelle Méditerranée contre tant de boue
Je sortirai crotté statue de lave,
boiteux par blessure à la hanche.
Je dirai aux hommes: «Tenez
votre part de dimanche!»

Tu n'entends pas leur rire
dit le Maître de l'Absolu,
tu ne vois pas le sang!

Entre les hommes et vous le sang coule
dit le Poète
et vous ne voyez plus
Moi dans les plaies je plongerai les mains
pour que le sang s'arrête
et chirurgien j'accepterai la douleur
les autres, et le remords,
afin que notre Corps total nous soit rendu.
Qu'importe ma pureté si elle n'est
point parmi les hommes!
Et si je ne pétris l'argile
que Dieu paisible en prendra soin

TO ALBERT CAMUS WHO CALLED ME A CUT THROAT

As for me, says the Poet,
my hands swirl around in the mud
hunting for dull stars.
Is there another way to raise them to the surface,
to turn them into diamonds,
to score the opaque windows?

Who will cleanse us, says the Master of the Absolute
what Mediterranean can counter so much mud.
I will go out covered in mud,
a statue of lava
limping from a wound at the thigh.
I will say to Man: "Here
is your share of Sunday!"

You don't hear them laughing
says the Master of the Absolute,
you don't see the blood!

The Poet says
blood is flowing between Man and you
and you no longer see
As for me, I will plunge my hands in the wounds
to stop the bleeding
and like a surgeon accept the pain
and remorse of others,
so that our Total Body can be returned to us.
If among men I am not pure,
what does my purity matter!
If I don't mold the clay
what peaceful God will tend to it

Piscines, stades, théâtres, livres
le Maître de l'Absolu se compose un décor d'oubli
Les absinthes, le sang de ses amis le hantent
Il invoque la mer, il interroge la mer
Tac! Tac!
Horloge! Mitraille!
Chaque seconde un homme tombe

Nous sommes investis du Verbe
pour pénétrer dans les charniers
crie le Poète.

Non, pas l'Homme
mais les hommes
avec leurs défauts et leurs puanteurs
et ce terrible appel du Christ en croix
lumière et peur!

Moi aussi dit le Poète
je rêve que l'eau et la terre
ne soient plus cette boue

Le Maître de l'Absolu
vers le gué de Jabbok riait au nez de l'Ami
Il gardait ses mains pures (ses icebergs!)
tandis que le Poète écrivait dans la frénésie
Et le Poète l'aimait.

Paris, 1-15 septembre 1956

Swimming pools, stadiums, theaters, books
the Master of the Absolute composes a backdrop of lapsed
    memory
The absinthes, the blood of his friends haunt him
He invokes the sea, he asks questions of it
Rat–a–tat!
Clock! Shots!
Every second a man falls

We are entrusted by the Word
to penetrate the charnel house
cries the Poet.

No, not Man
but men
with their faults and their stench
and that terrifying call from Christ on the cross
light and fear!

As for me, says the Poet,
I also dream that this water and land
might no longer be mud

The Master of the Absolute
near Jabbok's Ford laughed in the face of the Friend
He kept his hands pure (his icebergs!)
while the Poet wrote frantically
And the Poet loved him.

Paris, September 1-15, 1956

CITOYENS DE LAIDEUR

Maudit trahi traqué
Je suis l'ordure de ce peuple
Le pédé l'étranger le pauvre le
Fermant de discorde et de subversion.
Chassé de tout lieu toute page
Où se trouve votre belle nation
Je suis sur vos langues l'écharde
Et la tumeur à vos talons.

Je ne dors plus je traîne j'improvise de glanes
Un soleil de patience Ici
Fut un peuple là meurent
Courage et conscience. Le dire
Palais de stuc Jeunesse et Beauté à l'image
Des complexes touristiques. L'écrire
Dénoncer le bluff Pour que naisse
De tant de rats fuyants un homme
Risquer le poème et la mort.

Reclus, D. 6 août 1972

256

CITIZENS OF MONSTROSITY

Accursed betrayed hunted down
I am this nation's bastard
The fag the foreigner the poor man the
Ferment of discord and subversion.
Driven from all the places and all the pages
Of your beautiful nation
I am on your lips the splinter
and the tumor in your heels.

I don't sleep I hang about I improvise a bouquet from bits
    and pieces
A sun of patience Here
Were a people there die
Courage and conscience. To speak of it
Stucco palaces Youth and Beauty in the image of
Tourist centers. To write about it
Denouncing their bluff So that
From so many fleeing rats a man is born
To risk poems and death.

Reclus Sun. August 6th 1972